SOUTHERN OHIO
LEGENDS & LORE

James A. Willis

THE
History
PRESS

Published by The History Press
Charleston, SC
www.historypress.com

First published 2022

Manufactured in the United States

ISBN 9781467151115

Library of Congress Control Number: 2022936634

For Beezer and Khashoggi.

Who said that your party was all over?

CONTENTS

CONTENTS

PREFACE

N ot much. What's new with you?"
That's usually the response I give when people ask me what I've been up to since the 2017 History Press release of *Central Ohio Legends & Lore*, the first book in what appears to be turning into a series. But one only must flip on the news, look outside or even just visit the local grocery store to see, firsthand, that a *lot* has changed—not just for me, but for society as a whole. In the immortal words of the late, great John Lennon, "strange days indeed." But something that I constantly reminded myself of through it all was that I was living through history. Weird history. The kind of weirdness that first drew me in many, many years ago.

As a child, I was attracted to weird stories and subjects. It started with the usual suspects—ghosts, UFOs, the Loch Ness Monster—but quickly spread to the point where if there was even a hint of strangeness to the tale, I wanted to hear it. I was especially fond of stories that had history embedded in them—dates, names, exact locations. Those were the aspects of the stories that made them "real" to me. But what would really make my strange and spooky heart flutter was whenever I'd come across a strange story that I hadn't heard before—a story about a person, place or event that was obscure and, in my mind, in danger of being lost to time. I felt something of a kinship to the people in those stories and felt it was my responsibility to save them from fading into obscurity. At first, I was simply "telling stories" to my family and friends, but that eventually turned into posting things on the Internet. Currently, it's writing about these stories in books, just like the one you're currently holding in your hands.

So, hop in, I'll drive. Next stop, southern Ohio.

ACKNOWLEDGEMENTS

This book would not have been possible without the help and support of so many people, including Jeff Craig; Hidden Ohio and Map in Black; Brandi Hymer, for always fielding my bizarre editorial questions; the late, great Richard Gill, for introducing me to the Elmore Rider; Daniel Gill; Steve and Carol Flee, for showing me the most indirect direct route from Oxford to Seven Mile; John Rodrigue and Ryan Finn at The History Press; the Hidden Marietta Tour Company; Mark Moran and Mark Sceurman, for being the first ones to allow me to explore my weird side; and everyone at The Ghosts of Ohio, for supporting my side hustle.

And once again, saving the best for last, none of this would have been possible without the love and support of Steph and Courtney, even if that meant waiting patiently in the car when things got too spooky.

PART I
GHOSTLY LEGENDS

Bloody Horseshoe Grave

Everyone loves a good ghost story. The ones that tend to rise above the rest are the ones that can be supported with evidence. Unfortunately, in the day and age of reality television and online streaming, what is often presented as evidence falls under the category of "Yeah, they totally faked that." Of course, there are exceptions. Case in point, the Otterbein Cemetery in Somerset, Ohio, where the evidence can literally be found on one of the tombstones. As to evidence of what, well, that's another story entirely.

As the story goes, a man by the name of James Henry had fallen in love with two different women—Mary Angle and Rachel Hodge. Unsure of which one to marry, James was so overcome with trying to answer that question that he would often hitch up his wagon late at night and take to the country roads to consider his situation. These late-night excursions would often last hours and sometimes ended with James falling asleep at the reins, as it were. When that happened, James's faithful horse (in some version of the story, the horse is called "Bob") would inevitably know the way home, and James would wake up outside the front door of his home.

One evening, as James thought himself to sleep and visions of marriage danced in his head, his horse journeyed on. And this time, when James woke up, he found that his horse had taken him to the house of Mary Angle. Taking it as a sign that he should marry Mary, James did exactly that, and the couple were wed on January 11, 1843. Some variations of the story have

Otterbein Cemetery, home of the bloody horseshoe grave. *Author photo.*

Bob the horse being present at the wedding, while others state James gave the horse to Mary as a wedding gift.

By all accounts, James and Mary were a happy couple. But the marriage would be short-lived, as Mary died in childbirth barely two years after their second wedding anniversary. Grief-stricken, James once again found himself alone, and I bet you know what happened next, right? You got it—James turned right around and asked Rachel Hodge to marry him. It is said that James gave Rachel Bob the horse as a gift on their wedding day—something that didn't sit well with Bob…or Mary's ghost.

Shortly after James and Rachel's wedding, people started claiming to have seen an eerie sight out at Mary's grave in Otterbein Cemetery. On the back of Mary's tombstone, the outline of a bloody horseshoe had appeared. Locals began taking it as an omen of bad things to come, particularly for James. James, however, shrugged the whole thing off.

One morning, James woke up and announced to Rachel that he was going out to the barn to hitch Bob up for a late-morning trip. When James didn't return from the barn for breakfast, Rachel went out looking for him. Upon entering the barn, the first thing Rachel saw was Bob the horse, standing in the center of the barn, a motionless body lying face-down at his feet. Rachel had found James, dead. Rachel ran to her husband and struggled to roll him over. When she did, Rachel was horrified to see an indentation in the middle of James's forehead: a mark in the shape of a horseshoe. As Rachel cried out in terror, Bob stood silently by and gazed down at the body of James Henry.

Today, even though the events of this story happened more than 250 years ago, it is said that if you make your way out to Otterbein Cemetery and locate Mary Angle's grave, a strange mark, resembling a bloody horseshoe, can be seen on the back of the stone. What's more, on certain nights, you may hear Bob's hoofbeats as he plods up and down the roads around Otterbein Cemetery.

Strange story, to be sure. But is there any truth to it? More importantly, where did the story originate? Interestingly enough, the story itself might have gotten its start from the tale's ending—namely, the tombstone at Otterbein Cemetery. The back of Mary Angle's tombstone does indeed have what appears to be a stain in the shape of a bloody horseshoe on it. I have visited the cemetery numerous times since 1999, and it's always there. It appears to be the same mark and does not exhibit any signs of fading or having been accentuated (redrawn, colored in and so on). The mark itself does not appear to have been drawn on, and if it truly was put there naturally, the best I can come up with is that the piece of the tombstone bearing the mark (the

The back of Mary's tombstone, complete with bloody horseshoe. *Author photo*.

tombstone itself is broken into several pieces and was put back together) fell or was placed on top of a horseshoe or similarly shaped metal object and said object rusted, causing the rust to create the outline.

But just because there's a mark on the back of the tombstone doesn't mean the rest of the story is true, right? Correct. So, let's take a closer look at the main characters in the story.

To begin with, all three humans in the story did exist, and many life events did occur as they do in the story. James Kennedy Henry, born on March 14, 1814, did indeed marry Mary Catherine Angle on January 11, 1843. Records indicate that Mary "died in childbirth," and the date of her death was February 28, 1845. James next married Rachel Van Sickle Hodge on December 7, 1848, almost three years after Mary's death. Death also does not come to James as swiftly as it did in the legend, as he died on April 8, 1859—after more than a decade of marriage to Rachel. I guess if the bloody horseshoe on Mary's grave was to be taken as some sort of harbinger of doom or of a curse, it sure took its time executing it!

In terms of where the story itself originated, the earliest form of it in print that I could find was in *Haunting Tales from Fairfield County*, an assortment of more than a dozen stories collected by the Fairfield County District Library in the early 1980s. The November 7, 1980 edition of the *Columbus Citizen-Journal* quoted Shay Baker, head of extension services for the Fairfield County District Library, as saying that the collecting of stories was being done as "part of an effort to preserve the area's local history." The article goes on explain that all the collected stories will be "analyzed by humanities scholars who will classify the folklore and how it links to the mainstream of folklore."

As it appears in *Haunting Tales from Fairfield County*, the story concerning James Henry is credited to James Heinzman. This telling—which, at least for now, is the original—contains most of the beats the current version has. A notable difference is that in Heinzman's version, Mary is described as an "avid horse lover" whose favorite pastime was to ride her favorite (albeit unnamed) horse. This is the horse that James gives to Rachel after Mary dies. This version gives a better explanation as to why people would hear a ghostly horse running around near the cemetery—it's Mary's ghost, doing what she used to do when she was alive. An interesting side note is that Heinzman's version includes James's ghost coming along for the spectral ride: "On foggy nights, you're supposed to be able to hear the hoof beats of him [James] and his first wife riding horses up Otterbein Road late at night."

Looking at all the individual facts surrounding this ghostly legend, it appears that the vast majority of them are rooted in historical fact. The only sticking point revolves around that bloody horseshoe-looking thing on the back of Mary's tombstone. In sort of a chicken-or-egg situation, it would be ideal if we could figure out which came first, the legend or the strange mark on the tombstone. At present time, that is proving a lot easier said than done. According to the Heinzman version, the bloody horseshoe was visible just prior to James's death, which was in 1859, and has remained ever since. However, Heinzman's story includes the line, "The tombstone has been replaced several times and always a bloody horseshoe comes back on it," which leads one to believe that there might be brief periods of time when there was no horseshoe visible on the back of Mary's stone. Heinzman's "tombstone has been replaced several times" comment might also be responsible for a bit of a wrinkle in the story.

In October 1986, Sue Daniels, staff writer for the *Lancaster Eagle-Gazette*, featured the bloody horseshoe legend in her article about local haunts. Quoting heavily from the Heinzman story, Daniels retold the story, ending it with a description of Mary's headstone and the line, "There appears to be no evidence of a horseshoe." At first glance, this would seem to point toward the horseshoe that's visible today being added (or appearing) after October 1986. However, it should be noted that while there is an uncredited photograph of Mary's tombstone accompanying the Daniels article, it is only of the front, making it possible that Daniels didn't actually visit the cemetery and was simply describing the photograph of the front. Or, if she did visit the cemetery, she never walked around to view the back of the stone.

A final note about Daniels's article is that it contains a rather lengthy explanation as to why a tombstone would break into pieces like Mary's has. Daniels even interviewed someone from Danison Monument Works Inc. to explain that "neglect and decay" can cause some tombstones to

Mary's tombstone shows signs of having been broken over the years. *Author photo.*

fall apart. It all comes across as a bit of a head scratcher until Daniels drops the line, "The tombstone of Mary Henry looks as though it has been kicked by a horse." Wait, what? Couple that statement with Daniels's line in the caption under the photo of the front of Mary's tombstone—"It is believed by the story's teller that Mary's horse revisits her grave to leave a bloody hoofprint"—and you might be left wondering if Daniels is trying to imply that the bloody horseshoe imprint is caused by the ghost of Mary's horse kicking the headstone. Aside from the fact that Mary's horse was still alive when the bloody horseshoe mark is said to have first appeared, there's no mention of the condition of Mary's tombstone in any other version than Daniels's.

While we're able to confirm most of the things in the "Bloody Horseshoe Grave" tale, some specifics continue to elude us. But perhaps that's exactly what allows certain ghost stories to survive—the inability to disprove it in its entirety. Well, that and the idea that there are certain aspects of this tale that you, the reader, can see and experience for yourself. So please, plan a visit to Somerset's Otterbein Cemetery and check out the back of Mary Henry's tombstone. See if there's anything there resembling a bloody horseshoe. And then, since all Ohio cemeteries close at dusk, take your leave and perhaps take a late-night stroll down the road, especially if the night turns foggy. Who knows? You might just hear a distant horse, riding up toward you. If that happens, you'll be one step closer to validating the legend. That is, provided you stick around long enough to see who or what is coming toward you.

A SAFE PLACE TO DROP ANCHOR

Some places are said to be haunted simply because they look like they *should* be haunted. The Anchorage is such a place. When one stares up at the Anchorage, perched on a hillside on the western side of Marietta, one can't help but picture a wayward spirit or two gliding past the windows or perhaps gazing back down at you from the tower of this beautiful yet foreboding sandstone structure. And wouldn't you know it, the Anchorage is indeed supposed to be haunted by several spirits. Unearthing just who is said to haunt this building entails first diving into the location's history, as the Anchorage is where history and ghost stories are said to coexist.

The man responsible for the creation of the Anchorage—in other words, the guy with all the money—was Douglas Putnam. Born on April 7, 1806, to parents David and Elizabeth, Douglas seemed to have the Midas touch, in that every business venture he engaged in was successful. He was so successful that it came to the surprise of no one when Putnam announced his plans to build his estate house atop a hill so that it could overlook both the Ohio and Muskingum Rivers, depending on which way one looked. What is often overlooked is that Putnam allegedly built the house specifically for his wife, Eliza.

For the design of his new home, Douglas Putnam chose local architect John Slocomb, who had designed several other high-profile houses and buildings in the area, including several churches. Slocomb chose to design the house in the Italianate style—a style characterized by, among other things, tall first-floor windows, flat or low-pitched roofs and eaves that extend away from the sides of the structure. Oh yes, and a cool tower, too.

At first glance, it might seem odd to design a house in the Italianate style in, of all places, southern Ohio, but closer inspection proves that it makes total sense. While Italianate architecture became popular in Europe in the 1840s, it made its way to the United States thanks in large part to architect Alexander Jackson Davis. The style quickly caught on in several areas of the country, including southern Ohio. In fact, today, one of the largest collections of Italianate buildings in the entire United States is located in Cincinnati's Over-the-Rhine neighborhood.

Construction on the building that would become known as Putnam's Villa, in keeping with the Italianate theme, began in the early 1850s. Built on a solid rock foundation, the house was constructed using locally sourced wood as well as sandstone quarried from the hill behind where the house was being built. But even with all those local resources, construction moved along at a snail's pace, and the Putnams didn't move into Putnam Villa until late 1859. But it is said that all good things come to those who wait, and this was certainly true here. The beautiful four-story home, complete with tower, featured more than twenty rooms, two-foot-thick walls, a marble fireplace, twelve-foot ceilings and even a walk-in closet, something unique for the time. As for the estate itself, original estimates put the property at close to nine acres. The total price tag was rumored to be about $65,000, which today would be well over $2 million. Perhaps that's why some locals began referring to the house as "Putnam's Folly."

By all accounts, Eliza loved her new home and took great pride in showing it off. Alas, less than three years after moving in, Eliza died in her home on September 9, 1862, losing her battle with heart disease. While Douglas Putnam would remarry several years after Eliza's death, he would continue living in Putnam Villa until his death on December 20, 1894. Putnam Villa was then sold to Harry D. Knox, who operated a local boat-building company. It was Knox who, in homage to the nautical industry that had allowed him to acquire the money to purchase the home, renamed

The Anchorage, taken during my 2018 overnight stay. *Author photo*.

it the Anchorage—a safe place to drop anchor. He was also responsible for creating a driveway in front of the home in the shape of an anchor.

After Harry Know, the Anchorage would pass through several different owners, including author Dorothy James Roberts. In 1918, the house and property were purchased by Edward E. MacTaggart, a very rich man who had made his money from Oklahoma oil wells. For the next thirty-plus years, MacTaggart invested time, money, artwork and antiques to restoring and refurnishing the Anchorage. When MacTaggart passed away in 1952, his sister, Sophia Russel, took ownership and lived at the Anchorage until she died in 1962. On July 24–25, 1963, an auction was held at the Anchorage, and the bulk of antiques and artwork Edward MacTaggart had furnished the house with were sold off. Shortly thereafter, it was announced that the home would be turned into a nursing home, the Christian Anchorage. With that, the days of the Anchorage being a private residence came to an end.

To function as a nursing home, certain changes needed to take place regarding the layout. Perhaps the most disturbing, albeit necessary, changes were that staircases had to be walled up and an elevator shaft created to go between the floors. Little by little, the warm, inviting aspects of the Anchorage were pulled down, replaced by cold, commercial-grade materials. Even with these changes, the building was no match for more modern facilities, and in 1984, the Christian Anchorage was vacated and all its current residents moved to a nearby facility. In March 1992, the building was purchased with the initial intent to use it as an affiliate of the Marietta Memorial Hospital. However, there was very little movement, and the Anchorage, by and large, sat abandoned until Marietta Memorial Hospital sold it to the Washington County Historical Society for one dollar. Since that sale, the society has been working tirelessly to return the Anchorage to its former glory. Tours of the building are offered, including ghost tours, which are given by the Hidden Marietta Tour Company.

Ah yes, the ghosts. So, who is haunting the Anchorage? Given the building's storied past, many ghostly candidates arise. And while the Anchorage has certainly acquired more than its fair share of "ghostly children giggling" and "shadow figures moving around" tales, the one person who is almost always brought up is the one who was there from the beginning: Eliza Putnam. Makes sense, after all, as the house was built for her, and after waiting almost a decade to move in, she was only able to enjoy it for a few short years. So, while some may claim to hear ghosts related to the nursing home years or even see Douglas Putnam himself in a top hat, make no mistake: the Anchorage is Eliza Putnam's home…even if she never even called it the Anchorage!

In 2018, I was honored to have the opportunity to spend the night inside the Anchorage with my group, The Ghosts of Ohio, as part of a private hunt. As per the norm, we were given a tour of the building and then broke into small two- to three-person groups. I had heard that the ghost they believe is Eliza is sometimes seen in the first-floor parlor and on the stairs. So, for the first part of the night, I chose to sit in the large room across from the parlor, since that would also put me close to the stairs. Darrin, one of the long-standing members of The Ghosts of Ohio, sat with me. Two other members, Wendy and Kathy, chose to sit in the parlor while the team of the team headed upstairs.

Staircase at the Anchorage, where visitors have reported ghostly happenings. *Author photo*.

As Darrin and I sat in the room, I started to get the feeling that there was nothing ghostly in this building. To be honest, I get that feeling a lot. I will spend months if not years researching a haunted location and get myself all worked up, and then, when I'm finally there, nothing happens. Not even a weird chill or quick feeling of dread—nothing. And sitting there that night inside the Anchorage, I felt nothing except warmth and calmness. Even in its "work in progress" state, the entire building felt somewhat cozy. Definitely not what I was expecting to feel.

Time went by, and after a few unsuccessful attempts to contact Eliza (or any other ghost that might have been lingering in the house), Darrin and I moved up to the front of the room, facing forward, and began having a conversation about whether we thought there were any ghosts with us right now. That's when I heard the noise from the back of the room.

It was clearly a woman's voice, making a noise that I can only describe as something one would do when trying to imitate a ghost. Sort of like a "ooooooooooooohhhhhhhhhhhhh," but with a tinge of comedy mixed in, almost as if they weren't really trying to scare us, but rather have a bit of fun with us.

I turned to Darrin and asked, "Did you hear that?," to which he replied that he did. Darrin then proceeded to describe exactly what I had just heard: a woman pretending to be a ghost. The noise was so loud that, initially, there was no doubt in our minds that we were bring pranked.

The noise had come from the back of the room, which was directly behind us. Facing that direction, there was an exterior wall to the right and a door to the hallway on the left. There was also a door leading to that same hallway right next to where we were standing, so we went out that door into the hallway, expecting to see a living, breathing woman standing there, smiling. Except the hallway was empty. We then crossed the hallway and went into the parlor, where Wendy and Kathy were—the only women other than our host on that floor. They seemed confused when Darrin and I asked if they had heard a woman cheekily pretending to be a ghost. They both said they didn't hear anything.

Now comes the weird part. There were multiple audio recorders in the room with Darrin and me when we heard the woman, including a studio microphone connected directly to a mixer and even a video camera (with, admittedly, an inferior internal microphone). But when all that audio and video was reviewed, no woman pretending to be a ghost presented itself. Simply put, there was nothing there. Leading up to the time we heard her, you can hear Darrin and me moving around in our chairs and occasionally talking. Then silence until you hear me say, "What was that? Did you hear that?" There's not even any noise that we perhaps could have mistaken for a woman. At the moment we heard the woman, there is nothing on audio or video except silence and the image of two men sitting in an otherwise empty room. And yet, Darrin and I both heard the exact same…something. Something so loud that we heard it plain as day with our own ears—so loud that we thought a woman was in the room with us. Except there was no woman in the room.

The recording devices also did not pick up any sounds that would indicate someone walking into and/or out of the door around the time we heard the noise. It was as if whatever made that sound was either in the room with us the whole time or somehow managed to come in and out without making a single sound.

For obvious reasons, I can't say that what Darrin and I encountered at the Anchorage was a ghost. I can only say that I know we heard something and that, years later, we're still struggling to find a rational explanation for it—something so loud that wasn't picked up by a single device that was recording in the room at the time. Plus, I really want it to be a ghost, if for no other reason that it never ceases to put a smile on my face to consider that that evening, a female ghost saw Darrin and me "hunting" and decided to have a little fun with us. I can almost see her thinking, "Okay, you want a ghost? I'll give you guys a ghost," and then making her semi-mocking ghost noise. If I ever were able to prove that, I would proudly proclaim to anyone who would listen that I was once openly mocked by a ghost.

Since I can't tell you that it was a ghost, I most certainly can't tell you that it was Eliza Putnam either. I will say that stories abound of Eliza loving to entertain. So perhaps that's what she was doing that night. Although one could make the point that she was just entertaining herself at our expense. Who knows? But they say that in order to prove the existence of ghosts, one needs provable, repeatable data. I've already told you where I was sitting when I heard the "sarcastic ghost." Now go ahead and plan a tour of the Anchorage for your very own, sit in that same spot and let me know if you hear anything!

GOING DOWN LICK ROAD

Imagine you're out driving around Colerain Township with friends some dark night, and they say they want to show you something down Lick Road. Your first reaction might be to start giggling uncontrollably like you were back in elementary school. Your laughter quickly ceases when your friend turns off West Kemper and onto Lick, for once you pass a few houses, Lick Road starts to feel like it's getting smaller and smaller. By the time you pass the "Road Ends" sign, you're fairly certain that this was a bad idea, and that's before Lick Road starts its sharp and sudden drop down into darkness.

When you reach the bottom of the hill, Lick Road simply stops, surrounded by trees, overgrown fields and several barred gates. You're pretty sure that you can see a path continuing off into the woods, but you're distracted by the sound of your friend turning off the car's ignition. Then, turning to you, they tell you the legend of Lick Road, starting by telling you this part of Lick Road isn't a safe place to be after dark, all because of what happened to Amy, the ghost that haunts this very spot.

Since I don't know any of your friends (at least I don't think I do), I'm not sure which version of the Lick Road legend they're going to tell you. Suffice to say, all versions center on a teenage girl named Amy, who in all tellings is murdered by someone "who was never caught." It's the specifics of the murder that vary. The most common version has Amy being raped and murdered inside a car parked at the end of Lick Road and her body being dumped there. A slight variation has Amy still being raped, but she manages to escape the car, running into the woods, where she is ultimately captured and murdered. One final version has Amy being murdered at

The end of Lick Road. *Author photo*.

The abandoned bridge near the end of Lick Road. *Author photo.*

another location and her body then dumped at the end of Lick Road. As mentioned, the big hook (urban legend pun intended) to all these versions is that the killer is never caught, implying that "he could still be out there right now, waiting."

Concerning Amy's ghost, while she is said to haunt the end of Lick Road, one could say that she does it with flair. Not content to simply float around the woods, there are reports of a ghostly woman crying out for help or even screaming, all while moving toward your car. If you're told one of the versions that involve Amy being attacked inside the car, a strange little ritual designed to help you make contact with Amy has been created. Legend has it that if you park your car at the end of Lick Road, lock it and then walk away for a bit, when you return, you'll find the inside of your windshield completely fogged up. Not only that, but if you look closely, you're supposed to find the words "help me" written in the condensation, from inside your locked car.

My file folder on Lick Road dates to 2004, which would have been the first time I heard the stories. I can distinctly remember my first visit to Lick Road, again in 2004...in broad daylight. Standing at the end of the road, all the legends running through my head, I was almost immediately ready to dismiss everything as just one big Lover's Lane cautionary tale. All the elements were there: an isolated place to park, a life cut short and, of course, a killer who is never identified and still might be prowling around, waiting for his next victim. But over the years, I've trained myself to never give up on a ghost story without at least doing a little research first. Sure, historical documentation (or the lack thereof) doesn't necessarily prove or disprove a haunting. At the very least, though, it could help you set the record straight or even allow you to see where the story got its start. With the Lick Road legend, it all hinged on one question: Who was Amy?

The first step was to see if there were any records regarding an Amy being murdered on Lick Road. I came up empty on that one. Next, I broadened my search to any recorded deaths on Lick Road by any means (murder, suicide, natural causes) and both male and female. Again, nothing. Officially, not a single person has died on Lick Road. Frustrated, I left Lick Road behind and broadened my search to include any deaths of any females within a ten-mile radius of Lick Road. That's when I first met Linda Dyer.

On August 24, 1978, the nude body of fifteen-year-old Linda Dyer was found along a creek bed off Bank Road in Colerain Township. She had a six-inch stab wound in her chest, and the coroner would later determine that there was evidence of attempted strangulation. Based on the lack of blood in the area surrounding Dyer's body, authorities concluded that she had been murdered elsewhere and her body placed there after the fact.

Dyer had last been seen in the early morning hours of August 22, getting into an orange Volkswagen with Ohio license plates and occupied by two men. Dyer had just left a party in Monfort Heights and was hitchhiking near North Bend Road when the men stopped and picked her up. Police interviews of everyone who attended the party that night determined that the men in the Volkswagen had not been at the party. It was unclear if Dyer knew either of the men. Despite a thorough investigation, the two men were never identified. To this day, no one has ever been officially charged for the murder of Linda Dyer.

Looking over my notes, while she's not named Amy, Linda Dyer still checks all the boxes related to the Lick Road story. She was a teenager who apparently had been attacked while in a car. And like Amy, Linda Dyer's killers were never apprehended. Authorities were also never able to determine exactly where Dyer was murdered, so this would have opened the legend up to include the isolated end of nearby Lick Road as a possible location. The fact that Dyer's body was recovered on Bank Road, which is only roughly one mile from Lick Road, felt like further evidence to me that Dyer was the Amy I was looking for. But there's more.

As it turns out, Linda Dyer was only one of several young women who had been murdered and had their nude bodies unceremoniously dumped in the area. No one was sure if there was a serial killer on the loose or even if the murders were connected, but everyone was talking about the crimes. Linda Dyer's name was almost always mentioned in those conversations. In fact, on December 29, in what appeared to be part of a "Year in Review" segment, WCPO-TV in Cincinnati ran an ad in the *Cincinnati Enquirer*, asking people to pick their top ten news stories for 1976, with the results being announced on the 11:00 p.m. news broadcast. One of the news stories to choose from was "Succession of slayings of young women, whose nude bodies were found in outer areas." Several of the women's names are listed, including Linda Dyer's.

It's apparent to me that Linda Dyer's murder was all Lick Road needed to become home to the ultimate urban legend/ghost story combo. Think about it: The area at the bottom of Lick Road is the perfect Lover's Lane—dark and isolated. It's been that way for many decades. Originally private property, in the late 1970s, it became Richardson Forest Preserve, named after Dr. Albert S. Richardson, longtime chemical research director for Proctor & Gamble. Richardson passed away on November 16, 1978, and the following February, his widow, Ann W. Richardson, donated 162 acres to Hamilton County in memory of her husband. Since then, the preserve has flourished and nearly tripled in size, ensuring that the end of Lick Road will remain isolated for many years to come. The reserve also closes every night at dusk, meaning anyone entering at night is trespassing. All in all, this makes the end of Lick Road exactly the type of place teens flock to and parents try to keep them out of, often using cautionary tales to do so. But that only serves to make the teens want to go there even more. It's the allure of danger. Add to that the reality that a murdered girl's body was recovered nearby and Lick Road easily becomes a breeding ground for urban legends and ghost stories.

But all of this doesn't mean there *aren't* ghosts on Lick Road. Granted, the ghost might not be named Amy (or Linda, for that matter). It just means more research needs to be done, which brings us back to the imaginary visit I asked you to envision at the beginning of this story. So, there you are, sitting at the end of Lick Road in the middle of the night. Are you getting out of the car? Rolling down the window and listening for the ghostly screams? Or are you asking your driver to start the car and get you out of there as quickly as possible?

DRIVING WHILE HEADLESS

Growing up in New York, it seemed inevitable that the first ghost story to capture my imagination was the Headless Horseman from Washington Irving's "The Legend of Sleepy Hollow." There was just something so exciting, so enthralling and so terrifying about a ghost that would stop at nothing to pursue you, even though he no longer had a head. Alas, as I grew older and really started venturing out to experience a true ghostly encounter, tales of headless specters became few and far between. I couldn't quite put my finger on why, although I suspected the decline was due in part to horses no longer being the preferred mode of transportation, even for people who still had their head. You can imagine my excitement, then, when I moved to Ohio in 1999 and learned that the Buckeye State was home to several headless ghosts. And in the case of the one in Oxford, Ohio, people were claiming to have caught a glimpse of him on a fairly regular basis.

As one drives through uptown Oxford, with its quaint shops, bars and restaurants, it's hard to imagine that this city is said to be home to a headless ghost—one that rides a motorcycle, no less. But get out beyond the campus, past the off-campus student houses with wooden, hand-painted names on them, and the landscape quickly changes. And once you've past your last streetlight, the darkened road will begin to twist and turn in front of you, to the point where you almost begin to dread what your headlights might pick up just around the next bend. By the time you make that turn onto Earhart Road, you'll be ready to believe just about anything.

The legend associated with this stretch of road has, like all good legends, changed over the years. The most popular version goes something like this: A teenage girl lived with her parents in a house at the bend where Earhart Road and Oxford-Milford Road meet. This girl fell head over heels in love with a teenage boy who lived with his parents farther down Oxford-Milford Road. By all accounts, the two were very much in love and seemed like the perfect match for each other. There was just one problem: the boy rode a motorcycle. For

Welcome to Oxford. Don't lose your head. *Courtesy of Courtney Willis.*

this very reason, the girl's parents said they didn't want her to continue seeing the boy. With tears in her eyes, the girl agreed to stop seeing the boy. But teenagers sometimes have a habit of disobeying their parents.

The teenage couple decided that they were going to continue to see each other, in secret, and devised a plan. Whenever the couple wanted to go out on a date, the girl would wait for her parents to go to bed. She would then flash the front porch light on her house three times, signaling her boyfriend. Once he saw the flashing light, he would leave his house and push his motorcycle down to the girl's house. When he arrived, the girl would sneak out of her house, hop on the motorcycle and the boyfriend would push the bike clear of her house before cranking it up and heading off into the night.

Their secret plan worked, for a while. But one night, after making plans earlier in the day to see each other, the boy fell asleep while waiting for his girlfriend to flash the porch light. When he woke up, he found that he had slept through the appointed date time. His girlfriend was also now frantically flashing the porch light. Since he was running so far behind, the boy decided to make up time by driving the motorcycle down to the house rather than pushing it. He also took off down Oxford-Milford Road at a higher rate of speed than usual, just so he could reach his girlfriend faster. Only problem was he was going far too fast for the hilly road, and when he reached the sharp turn in front of his girlfriend's house, he lost control of the motorcycle, veering wildly off the road and into a field. Unfortunately for the young man, the field was enclosed by a barbed wire fence, which he crashed through headfirst…and came out the other side minus his head—he had hit the fence at such a high rate of speed that it sheared his head clean off at the neck.

Today, even though the girlfriend's parents' house no longer stands, people still drive out to the sharp bend where Earhart Road and Oxford-Milford come together, face their car down Oxford-Milford Road and flash their headlights three times, mimicking the girlfriend's flashing of the porch light so many years ago. Legend has it that sometimes, that flashing message will be received by a long-dead teenager, who will hop aboard his spectral motorcycle, mistaking you for his girlfriend. When that happens, you are supposed to be able to see the headlight from his motorcycle, coming down Oxford-Milford Road toward you. But just before the light reaches you, it blinks out and vanishes, almost as quickly as it appeared.

It's a great story, but hardly any of it can be historically verified. No accident, no deaths, not even a record of a house ever being in the field where the girlfriend's house was supposed to have stood (although my wife,

The junction of Oxford-Milford and Earhart: ground zero for the Oxford Rider. *Author photo.*

Steph, who grew up in Oxford, swears there was one there). I was able to find a single report of a fatal motorcycle accident in the area. The single-vehicle accident did involve a young man and did result in his death, but that's where the similarities end. The accident took place several streets over from Oxford-Milford Road and happened in broad daylight, and while there were head injuries involved, they were the result of the operator not wearing a helmet, not because of a barbed wire fence. The story isn't all that old, as far as ghost stories go, as I've only been able to trace it back to the mid-1970s. So how did this story come to be?

If I had to guess, I'd say that the Oxford Motorcycle Ghost got its start from another headless motorcycle ghost in Ohio: the Elmore Rider.

Located almost two hundred miles northeast of Oxford—so basically on the opposite end of the state—the town of Elmore sports a headless motorcyclist story that predates the Oxford version by decades. In the Elmore version, a young man returning from "the war" rides his motorcycle over to his girlfriend's house, only to find her in the arms of another man. Speeding away in a fit of rage, the man crashes his motorcycle while crossing a bridge, losing his head in the process. For a chance to see the Elmore Rider, one needs to park their car and flash the headlights three times, at which point the ghostly light from the rider's headlight will come toward them. Perhaps the biggest difference between the two legends is that in Elmore, you can only see the ghost light on the anniversary of the crash, March 21.

As mentioned, urban legends and ghost stories often mutate over time, which is something that tends to keep the best tales going. If one looks at the Elmore story, the basic elements of the Oxford story are there: boyfriend-girlfriend rendezvous, a motorcycle accident resulting in decapitation, even the flashing of headlights three times to summon the spirit. It's interesting to note that the Elmore Rider story can be traced back to a time when there wasn't even a motorcycle involved, just a "ghost light" coming down the road. Truth be told, the Elmore Rider legend was in danger of fizzling out if not for one man, Bowling Green State University alum Richard Wayne Gill. In 1968, Gill and a friend, who wished to remain anonymous, ventured out in search of the Elmore Rider. According to Gill, the two were not only able to summon the rider several times, but at one point, the friend also decided to stand in the middle of the road to see what would happen. The result was the light launching the friend off to the side of the road, where Gill found him, unconscious—an event that certainly explains why Gill's friend wished to remain anonymous.

Richard Gill, who I had the absolute honor of meeting and chatting with years ago after one of my presentations in Bowling Green, was, among other things, an avid folklorist, so much so that he wrote about his encounter in the December 1972 edition of the *Ohio Folklore Society Journal*. The journal was published by the society at The Ohio State University in Columbus and distributed to other university across Ohio, including Miami University in Oxford.

Driving down Oxford-Milford Road, hoping to see "the light." *Author photo.*

So, now we have a possible route the headless motorcycle ghost stories might have traveled to get to Oxford. But why did this story take up residence on Oxford-Milford Road, especially since there are no records of any fatalities involving a motorcycle on this road? The answer to that is simple: lucky drivers on Oxford-Milford Road will actually see the light!

Hard to believe, but it is true. And I can attest to the fact that I have been driving up and down Oxford-Milford Road—all the way to the end of Earhart Road and back—for more than two decades and have seen a light that I have yet to explain. Occasionally, I have seen it when I'm driving all alone, but most of the time, there are others with me. My wife and daughter have seen it with me, as have both my father- and mother-in-law. I've seen it at different times in the evening, on different days of the week and in all types of weather. The only constants are that the light is always on the same side of Oxford-Milford Road, heading north toward Earhart Road, and it disappears before it reaches my car. The best way to describe the light is that it looks just like a headlight on the front of a motorcycle in that it's always in the center of the road. The light also appears to be giving off its own light, as it illuminates the road in front of it as it gets closer. And there's never any sound. I've also never been able to make out any sort of shape behind the light. It's just a light moving toward you before suddenly blinking out. I don't always see it when I go, but when I do, it is visible for ten to twenty seconds— long enough for my passengers to take videos and photos.

Over the years, I have been able to rule out most of the common "normal" explanations for the light: headlights from a distant car, reflectors on or along the road or neighboring house lights. The one thing I haven't been able to figure out is exactly what the light is. The not knowing is exactly why, in my opinion, the legend of the Headless Motorcycle Ghost came home to roost in Oxford in some sort of weird chicken-or-egg scenario. I believe people in Oxford knew of the light, but there was no story attached to it. Maybe it was just looked on as some weird, naturally occurring phenomenon. Then, someone read Richard Gill's Elmore Rider story in 1972's *Ohio Folklore Society Journal* and thought, "This light sounds like what people see out on Oxford-Milford Road." And that, as they say, is how legends are born.

PART II
LEGENDARY CHARACTERS

EUGENE: THE MAN NOBODY KNEW

On the morning of June 5, 1929, a stranger passed through the village of Sabina. No one paid much attention to the solitary figure walking east on the 3-C Highway, other than to note that he didn't appear to be from the area. Under normal circumstances, a stranger in the village would arouse suspicion, but this man was walking on the 3-C Highway, the only state route in Ohio to enter all three of the state's largest cities—Cincinnati, Columbus and Cleveland (hence the "3-C")—so it was not uncommon to see strangers passing through, even those on foot.

The following day, the body of an unidentified Black man, between fifty and sixty years of age, was found leaning against a fence post along the 3-C Highway, just west of Borum Road and about a mile east of Sabina. Later reports would claim that the man was "very relaxed and sort of thoughtful-looking," appearing as though he had passed away while sitting down to rest. Authorities were notified, and the closest funeral home, Littleton Funeral Home in Sabina, was contacted to come retrieve the body. Before the body was taken to the funeral home, police checked the man's meager belongings but found nothing that identified who he was. The only clue was a scrap of paper with a Cincinnati street address on it. Jotting down the address—1118 Yale Avenue—police hypothesized that if this was the address the man was coming from, coupled with the fact that it appeared the man was traveling east when he passed away, the stranger would have passed through Sabina at some point. Police then decided to follow the body back to Sabina and see if anyone recalled seeing the man.

A few Sabina residents did recall seeing the man passing through, but no one recognized him or could even say for sure if he had been traveling alone or with a companion. One Sabina resident did claim to have seen the stranger, remarking that it looked like "he was having trouble walking." Having hit a dead-end in Sabina, the decision was then made to try the Cincinnati address to see if there was anyone there who could identify the man. While authorities headed south, the Littleton Funeral Home was asked to have the body embalmed, pending notification of next of kin. Olin R. Moon of the Littleton Funeral Home was the one tasked with embalming the body.

In Cincinnati, authorities were met with another dead-end when the address found on the dead man was of a vacant lot, surrounded by houses on all sides. (Side note: it struck this author as odd that even today, that address is still vacant.) Neighbors were interviewed, but no one could provide any information about the identity of the man whose body was sitting inside the Littleton Funeral Home. Authorities were forced to return from Cincinnati empty-handed and no closer to identifying the man.

Back at the funeral home, Olin Moon had finished the embalming, dressed the man in a suit and placed the body in a small outbuilding. While it is true that the body was put "on display," the plan, at least initially, was that someone would be able to identify the man or at least provide a clue as to who he was. It was around this time that people started referring to the man by name: Eugene. While there is some confusion as to exactly where the name originated—some claim it came from the fact that the man living closest to the empty lot in Cincinnati was named Eugene Johnson—others say it was a random name chosen by Olin Moon and the Littleton family. Regardless, the name stuck, and before long, everyone was called the man Eugene.

Days turned into months, months into years, and still no one came to identify Eugene. But whenever some came through Sabina, they were encouraged to stop by the little brick building next to the Littleton Funeral Home to see if they could identify the man lying in the coffin. As Sabina was situated along the 3-C Highway, the major north–south route through Ohio, more and more people started stopping in Sabina, and Eugene quickly turned into a bit of a tourist attraction. While many came to view Eugene to try to identify him, others came because of ghoulish curiosity. Olin Moon had done such a good job embalming the body that rumors began to spread that Eugene was mummified, which also increased foot traffic through the small brick building. During World War II, chartered buses taking Selective Service members from southern Ohio up to Fort Hayes in Columbus for their physical exams would stop to refuel in Sabina. At peak operation, three to four buses per day would stop in Sabina, and every recruit, inevitably, would wander over for a peek at Eugene.

Through it all, the Littleton Funeral Home was still hoping that someone would step forward and positively identify Eugene, going so far as to install guest registration books next to Eugene's body. Staff also took steps to ensure that Eugene always looked his best for visitors, including fitting Eugene with a new suit to wear every year. They truly cared about Eugene. There was a moment in time, however, when they made a decision that, looking back, they would probably regret. That decision came in 1946, when Eugene was taken on a short tour around Ohio, stopping at local farmers' markets and even the Circleville Pumpkin Show, where interested parties could pay twenty-five cents to view the body of Eugene. From this point forward, some people started to look at Eugene as nothing more than a sideshow attraction.

When Eugene made his way back to Sabina, the Littleton Funeral Home noticed that people were no longer content to simply view the body. Now they wanted to physically touch it, often daring each other to do so. There were even morbid souvenir collectors who would attempt (sometimes successfully) to pull off a portion of Eugene's clothing or even, if reports are to be believed, the gold tooth from Eugene's mouth. The funeral home had to resort to putting up fencing so that visitors couldn't physically touch Eugene anymore. But the worst was still yet to come.

In the early morning hours of November 12, 1958, Elige Kellum, an Ohio State University employee, was making his way across campus when something caught his eye. At first, it appeared as though a man in a suit had fallen asleep on one of the campus benches. As Kellum drew closer, however, he realized that the man wasn't sleeping—he was dead. And by the looks of it, the man had been dead for some time. Kellum immediately contacted the authorities. One of the officers who arrived on scene recognized the man on the bench almost immediately. It was Eugene from Sabina, Ohio. Newspapers would later recount that "by 8:30 am, Eugene was back home, much to the relief of Bart Littleton, operator of the Littleton Funeral Home."

It would take weeks before police were able to piece together how Eugene had managed to make the hour-long journey up from Sabina to the Ohio State University campus. As it turns out, on the evening of November 11, five OSU students somehow managed to sneak into the small brick house that had become Eugene's home and abscond with the body. They then

Above: Entrance to Sabina Cemetery, Eugene's final resting place. *Author photo*.

Right: Eugene's grave at Sabina Cemetery. *Author photo*.

drove with it back to campus, leaving Eugene propped up on the bench where he would be found the following morning. Of the five students, OSU expelled four of them while choosing to only suspend the fifth. This would prove to be the beginning of the end of Eugene being available for public viewing. It would also be what made the Littleton Funeral Home finally come to the realization that no one was coming to claim poor Eugene. It was time to let him rest in peace.

At 9:00 a.m. on October 21, 1964, Eugene was finally laid to rest at Sabina Cemetery. The headline of the local newspaper read, "Eugene, the Man Nobody Knew, Was Buried Here Today." To avoid publicity, the Littleton Funeral Home did not announce the interment plans, and the service was kept to a small group of individuals, including Dr. F.M. Wentz, pastor of the local Methodist church, who conducted the service. The Littleton Funeral Home paid for the interment as well as the tombstone, which bore the name Eugene in quotes. Originally, the stone incorrectly listed Eugene's death year as 1928, leading to some confusion as to when his body had been found. The date was corrected and the stone currently in place reads, in its entirety:

> *"Eugene"*
> *Found dead 1929*
> *Buried 1964*

Today, Eugene's grave has become a travel destination for many, some of whom leave behind small trinkets out of respect for Eugene. In a strange way, it seems only fitting that an unknown man who once walked through Sabina, alone and unnoticed, would become the village's most famous resident.

"I Declare the Earth Is Hollow and Habitable Within"

The idea that planet Earth could be hollow is certainly not a new one. It has existed for centuries in one shape or form. But John Symmes Jr. added a unique wrinkle to the Hollow Earth theory—the notion that if you knew where to look, you could find entrances into the earth which would lead you to an inner area, occupied by all sorts of wildlife. What's more, there are remains of Symmes's theory in southern Ohio, but once again, you must know where to look.

There is very little in Symmes's upbringing that would suggest he would spend most of his adult life trying to raise funds for an expedition to find a hole in earth. Born John Cleves Symmes on November 5, 1780, to parents Thomas and Mercy, Symmes's early years were considered "normal," and he received "a good common English education." It's unclear if it was a career move or not, but in 1802, Symmes joined the U.S. Army, obtaining a commission as an ensign. He rose through the ranks, and by 1807, he had been promoted to first lieutenant. The following year, Symmes married Mary Anne Lockwood, a widow with six children. Symmes remained in the army through the War of 1812 and was promoted to captain before being honorably discharged in 1815.

After that, Symmes decided to go into business for himself as a trader, operating near St. Louis, Missouri. By all accounts, that didn't work out too well for him, but there was still nothing to suggest that Symmes was researching Hollow Earth theories or developing his own ideas. The first recorded mention by Symmes about his theory is in a letter sent to a relative in 1817, which included a passing mention of a hollow Earth. But even then, Symmes was clearly contemplating something bigger. He not only believed in the Hollow Earth theory, but he also had a new take on it: he believed that there were passageways into the earth, and he wanted to find those entrances. Of course, to do that, you're going to need money to fund an expedition—money Symmes didn't have. On top of that, no one knew anything about Symmes's theory.

After much thought, Symmes came up with a way that he thought would kill two birds with one stone. Symmes would write up his take on the Hollow Earth theory—his declaration—and then send it out to potential investors. Using his own money, Symmes printed up as many copies of his declaration as he could afford—five hundred copies—and then had it sent to "each notable foreign government, reigning prince, legislature, city, college, and philosophical societies, throughout the union, and to individual members of our National Legislature."

Dated April 10, 1818, Symmes's *Circular No. 1* began with the following proclamation:

> *To All the World!*
> *I declare the earth is hollow and habitable within; containing a number of solid concentrick spheres, one within the other, and that it is open at the poles 12 or 16 degrees; I pledge my life in support of this truth, and am ready to explore the hollow, if the world will support and aid me in the undertaking.*

Circular No. 1 then went on to lay out Symmes's theory in detail. Essentially, Symmes believed that Earth was made up of five concentric circles, like hollow spheres, each inside the other as if they were round nesting dolls. This in and of itself was also not a new theory. The new angle Symmes provided was that there were two openings into the Hollow Earth—one at the North Pole and the other at the South Pole, each thousands of miles wide. No one had proposed such a thing before, and these openings would come to be known as "Symmes Holes."

Symmes postulated that if one of the openings were entered, you could literally pass through all the inner spheres, eventually coming out on the opposite side of the planet. What's more, rather than being dark and gloomy inside Earth, Symmes believed that each of the spheres was brightly lit, the result of sunlight reflecting off the surface above it, all the way down to the center, on both sides of Earth. Because of this, Symmes believed the Hollow Earth created the perfect environment for all sorts of life to thrive and publicly stated that inside Earth was a "warm and rich land, stocked with thrifty vegetables and animals if not men."

Unfortunately for Symmes, *Circular No. 1*, did not get the reaction he was planning for when he published it. He was so confident that money from backers would come rolling in, even from entire nations, but it didn't. There was mild interest, but by and large, *Circular No. 1* was met with laughter, with more than a fair share of ridicule being directed at Symmes. Undeterred, Symmes and his family relocated to Newport, Kentucky, the following year and made plans to get backing for his expedition another way.

In 1820, Symmes soon came to the realization that in order to make his expedition a reality, he was going to have to defend his theory regarding Symmes Holes. Printing *Circular No. 1* didn't work, so Symmes decided that he needed to take his theory directly to the people. So, he made plans to embark on a series of speaking engagements, beginning in Newport, Kentucky, and Cincinnati, Ohio, where he could discuss his theory in greater detail. And who knows, maybe someone hearing him speak would be so impressed that they would open their wallet and happily finance a trip to one of the Symmes Holes.

For these presentations, even though Symmes was already in debt, he paid to have a custom wooden model of Earth constructed, showing how his theory was plausible. Symmes also simplified his original theory a bit. Gone were the five concentric circles, replaced by only one—making it a true hollow Earth. Sadly, even these tweaks didn't help, as it soon became apparent that Symmes was not a very good public speaker. He had a hard time articulating himself and would also stumble through the presentations, neither of which is a good thing when you're trying to convince people to give you money. But Symmes was able to acquire some followers who attended a presentation and walked away believers. One of those, Richard M. Johnson, met with Symmes and told him that they should petition Congress for the expedition money. Symmes agreed, and on March 7, 1822, Richard Johnson officially presented Symmes's petition to Congress. It was met with some interest, but after much discussion, Congress decided to table the petition and return to it at an undetermined time.

Due to Symmes's failing health, he would often invite some of his converts to speak at his presentations. One of these was Jeremiah Reynolds, who joined Symmes around 1824. It is said that Reynolds was directly responsible for the alleged presentation that took place before members of John Quincy Adams's cabinet regarding an expedition to the North Pole. Legend has it that there was serious interest but that they asked for more time.

Another of Symmes's followers who stepped in to help was James McBride. He was pushing Symmes to publish his theories, but Symmes was so strapped for cash that it was out of the question. That's when McBride took it upon himself to publish *Symmes' Theory of Concentric Spheres* in 1826. Still, there were no takers, and so the speaking engagements continued, further affecting Symmes's health. It is said that Symmes still clung to the idea that the Adams administration would be contacting him to say it was ready to back his expedition. That never happened, and when Adams lost his bid for reelection to Andrew Jackson in March 1829, that brought those dreams to an end; Jackson wanted nothing to do with finding Symmes Holes.

On May 28, 1929, John Cleves Symmes died, essentially penniless and without ever having proved his Symmes Holes existed. He was buried in southern Ohio at the Hamilton Burying Ground, which had been established back when the town of Hamilton was first laid out in the 1790s. Many thought that Symmes's Hollow Earth theory would be buried with him, but Jeremiah Reynolds was not willing to let go that easily.

After another brief and unsuccessful attempt to get Andrew Jackson to back an expedition, Reynolds began looking for other potential backers. In New York, Reynolds was able to convince a Dr. Watson to finance a trip to the South Pole to attempt to find the southern opening into the earth. In October 1829, Jeremiah Reynolds and Dr. Watson climbed aboard the *Annawan* with a year's worth of provisions and a full crew and set sail toward Antarctica, looking for a hole that would lead them inside the planet.

The Symmes Monument, complete with hollow Earth on top. *Author photo.*

As the *Annawan* neared Antarctica, they discovered what they would later describe as a "southern continent," completely blockaded with ice. A group of twenty men launched and managed to reach shore. They remained there for ten days, during which they were not able to locate any opening into the

Historical plaque at Symmes Park. *Author photo.*

South Pole and eventually discovered that they were eight degrees away from the South Pole. Returning to the *Annawan*, everyone gathered, and most of the crew were convinced they were not going to find any opening. They wanted to go home. Several days later, the crew mutinied. It ended with Dr. Watson and Jeremiah Reynolds being thrown off the boat at Valparaíso, Chile, and left there. So ended Reynolds's attempt to prove Symmes's theory.

There is a final postscript to John Symmes's story. In 1848, Hamilton, Ohio, created a new cemetery, Greenwood Cemetery, about four miles from the Hamilton Burying Ground, where John Symmes was buried. The decision was made to relocate the majority of bodies from the burying ground to Greenwood Cemetery. When the time came, all the bodies were indeed moved—all except one. John Symmes was allowed to stay, and a metal fence was placed around the grave. In 1873, Symmes's son, Americus, had a monument erected over his grave, complete with a hollow Earth sitting on top of it. Two Symmes Holes can be seen, one on either end, on the hollow Earth sphere. Today, that monument is still visible, along with a historical marker about John Symmes and his version of the Hollow Earth theory. Several years ago, the area where Symmes's grave is located was officially renamed Symmes Park.

Roy Rogers, King of the Cowboys

Entire generations of Americans grew up watching and listening to Roy Rogers, the King of the Cowboys. Known for his clean-cut image and soothing voice, his legions of fans flocked to movie houses, radios and television screens to ride along as a real-life cowboy from Wyoming chased down bad guys and righted wrongs, usually with the help of his trusty steed, Trigger. What no one suspected was that this great American cowboy was the creation of Hollywood executives, right down to his name. What's more, he got his start far away from Wyoming, along the Ohio River in southern Ohio.

The man who would become King of the Cowboys was born Leonard Franklin Slye on November 5, 1911, to parents Andy and Mattie. At the time of Leonard's birth, the family was living in a tenement house located at 412 Second Street in downtown Cincinnati. Decades later, the building would be demolished to make way for Riverfront Stadium, home of the NFL's Cincinnati Bengals and, more famously, the Cincinnati Reds baseball team. This would lead Leonard to joke in his later years that he was born "somewhere between second base and center field."

Just months after Leonard was born, Andy Slye decided that he and his family needed a change of scenery and made plans to move. But this was to be no ordinary move. With the help of his brother, Andy built a twelve-by-fifty-foot houseboat out of salvaged wood. Once it was completed, Andy loaded his family on board and floated southeast down the Ohio River to Portsmouth, Ohio, where Andy had purchased property.

Upon arriving in Portsmouth, the family continued to live on the houseboat while they began construction on their new home. But less than a year later, the Ohio River overflowed its banks by several feet in what became known as the Great Flood of 1913, forcing the Slye family to continue living on the houseboat longer than they expected. It wasn't all for naught, though, as when the waters finally receded, Andy Slye decided to just moor his houseboat permanently on his property, and that became the family home.

Several years later, Andy Slye decided that it was time for another change. This time, he moved his family north of Portsmouth to an area known as Duck Run, Ohio. Purchasing a farmhouse and close to eighty-seven acres, Andy's original intent was to become a farmer and use the farm as his only source of income. It didn't take long for him to realize that was going to be next to impossible, and in 1919, Andy was forced to take a job at a shoe factory to supplement his income. However, the job was not in town, meaning that the patriarch of the Slye family would be away from the farm for extended periods of time, often not returning home for two to three weeks at a time. That meant that most of the farm duties fell to the only other male member of the Slye family, Leonard, who was barely eight years old at the time.

Even with the help of his three sisters and his mother, life on the farm was hard for Leonard. But he did the best with what he had to work with and always approached things with a positive attitude. Living on a rural farm meant that the Slye family often had to rely on themselves for entertainment, which they were more than happy to do by having sing-alongs and taking turns playing an old mandolin. Leonard even taught himself to yodel. And when they really wanted to party it up, the Slye family would invite people out to their farmhouse for square dances, where the rest of the Slye family performed the music while Leonard called the square dances.

When Andy Slye came home from his job, he would often bring gifts for the family with him. On one occasion, he brought the family an old racehorse, Babe, to help around the farm. While one has to wonder how much help a former racehorse would be on a farm, Babe was instrumental in helping Leonard learn the basics of horsemanship.

Leonard attended high school in nearby McDermott, Ohio, but often found himself falling asleep in class due to his farm work taking up so much of his time. He managed to complete his sophomore year before deciding to drop out and take a job working alongside his father at the shoe factory. Try as he might, Leonard just couldn't get into his work at the shoe factory. Hearing his son talk about wanting a new job was all it took for Andy Slye to consider moving again. Since his daughter Mary had recently married and move to California, Andy Slye suggested that he and Leonard make a trip out west. Maybe there were better job opportunities out there, and if so, they could relocate the rest of the Slye family. In late 1929, Andy and Leonard Slye packed whatever they could into the family's 1923 Dodge and headed west to California. It would take them almost two weeks to make the trip.

Once they arrived, Andy and Leonard Slye found that jobs were incredibly scarce in California, due mainly to the start of the Great Depression. Leonard lasted only a few months in California before deciding to move back to Ohio. Reuniting with the harsh Midwest winters made Leonard Slye reach the conclusion that if he was going to look for work anywhere, he preferred the warmer climate of California, so he once again headed west, vowing to make it work no matter what it took.

Back in California, Leonard accepted any job he could find—from driving a gravel truck to picking peaches for Del Monte—to try to make ends meet. All the while, he still found time to visit his family for an evening of singing and mandolin playing, just like they had done back in Ohio. It is said that it was during one of these gatherings that Leonard's sister Mary suggested he try to get on *Midnight Frolic*, a radio program broadcast out of Inglewood, California, that featured local talent. Even though he was barely eighteen and "scared to death," Leonard thought that an appearance might lead to some paying gigs, so he went to the station and was able to land a spot on the program. Several days after appearing on the program—during which Leonard sang, played guitar and even yodeled—he received a call from Ebb Bowen, who asked Leonard to join his band, the Rocky Mountaineers. Leonard accepted, thus beginning his show business career.

The Rocky Mountaineers didn't last very long, though, and Leonard went and joined another group, the International Cowboys. Like the Rocky Mountaineers, the International Cowboys didn't last long either. It was at this point in his career that Leonard began developing a pattern where if a band he was in folded, he would just take a few of its members with him and form a new band. Leonard continued this pattern for the next few years, eventually forming the Sons of the Pioneers. It was with this band that Leonard Slye got his first break in motion pictures, appearing in several films in 1935 and 1936 as a band member. For those movies, he was credited as Len Slye. In 1937, Len Slye adopted the stage name Dick Weston.

While Dick Weston continued to hone his craft, America was busy falling in love with a new movie star, Gene Autry. Autry, who had made a name for himself as the Singing Cowboy, already had many hit records to his name when he begun making appearances in motion pictures put out by Republic Pictures Inc. Every movie Autry appeared in became an instant smash. That's why, in 1938, Autry demanded more money to appear in his next upcoming film, tentatively entitled *Washington Cowboy*. Never ones to willingly part with their money, Republic Pictures executives instead began to mull over the idea of finding the next singing cowboy to use in the film instead of Gene Autry. They settled on Leonard Franklin Slye from Cincinnati, Ohio. Of course, they'd have to make a few changes first.

The first was Slye's name. "Leonard Slye" just didn't have a nice ring to it. "Dick Weston" wasn't much better. So using the surname of another famous cowboy entertainer, the recently deceased Will Rogers, as a starting point, executives created Roy Rogers.

Next, executives felt that they needed to change their new cowboy's backstory. The idea of a cowboy who hailed from southern Ohio wasn't something they thought would play well with audiences. That's when Republic Pictures came up with something that hadn't been done before: they would create an entirely fictitious backstory for their new star and pass it off in publicity materials as being factual. So, in 1938, when Republic Pictures released *Under Western Stars*, the renamed and reworked *Washington Cowboy*, it introduced a new cowboy, Roy Rogers, who was born and raised on a cattle ranch in Wyoming before being discovered. Audiences went wild, never suspecting that everything they were being told about this new cowboy hero was a work of fiction, right down to his name.

Under Western Stars was a hit at the box office, and America wanted more of this singing cowboy Roy Rogers. Republic Pictures was more than happy to give them just that. Before 1938 had ended, three more movies starring Roy Rogers were released, including *Billy the Kid Returns*, which featured Roy Rogers playing both "himself" and Billy the Kid. From 1938 forward, whenever Leonard Slye appeared in a film, it was always as "Roy Rogers," even in films where he was portraying other characters. For example, 1940's *The Carson City Kid* was promoted as "starring Roy Rogers as the Carson City Kid."

In 1942, the name Leonard Slye was officially put out to pasture when he had it legally changed to Roy Rogers. The following year, *King of the Cowboys* was promoted, with ads declaring, "Roy Rogers is the King of the Cowboys." Indeed he was. By this point in his career, Roy Rogers had appeared in nearly forty movies, with Republic Pictures putting out seven to eight films per year, all of them hits. Roy now even had a faithful stallion, Trigger, which not only appeared in the movies with him but also accompanied him to public appearances, much to the delight of audiences. In 1944, Roy Rogers appeared in *The Cowboy and the Senorita* alongside actress Frances Smith, who was credited as Dale Evans. The two fell in love and were married on New Year's Eve 1947. The couple began making movies together, and altogether, they appeared in thirty-five films together, most while sharing the bill with Trigger.

Looking back, it is easy to see why America took to Roy Rogers. On screen, he epitomized what most people imagine when they think of an American hero. Things that are considered cliché today about our celluloid protagonists—showing up in the nick of time, riding off into the sunset, never killing anyone (Roy Rogers was famous for shooting guns out of bad guys' hands), even always wearing a white hat—were all brought to life by

Roy Rogers. As for the movies themselves, the violence in them was almost nonexistent and the subject matter such that parents felt comfortable letting their children watch them. The fact that Roy would often burst into song during the movies also meant that adults didn't mind sitting through a Roy Rogers film. Roll all of that together and it's no surprise that from the moment he was crowned King of the Cowboys in 1943, Roy Rogers was considered the biggest box office draw of all the cowboy and western movie stars.

Of course, Roy Rogers's appeal wasn't reserved just for the silver screen. Roy was one of a very select number of actors who can claim to have not only had a successful movie career but also a successful television show and radio show to boot. Then there was the Roy Rogers merchandise. While movie and television tie-in merchandise is commonplace today, that was not so much the case back in the 1940s and '50s. But that didn't stop Roy Rogers's likeness from appearing on everything from shirts, boots and hats to pajamas and jackets. In most cases, consumers could pick from a vast array of designs and decide if they wanted just Roy Rogers on it or if they wanted something with Roy, Trigger and Dale included too. People couldn't get enough, and soon there were Roy Rogers alarm clocks, watches, cookies, cameras, action figures, play sets, toy guns and comic books. At

Sears, for all your Roy Rogers–themed apparel. *From the* Bakersfield Californian, *Friday, August 19, 1949.*

Roy Rogers, King of the Cowboys, dead at 86

As news of Roy Rogers's passing spread, headlines were sure to remind everyone he was cowboy royalty. *From the* Daily Spectrum, *Tuesday, July 7, 1998.*

the height of his career, it was not uncommon to see department stores devoting entire newspaper ads to nothing but Roy Rogers merchandise. At one point, Roy Rogers merchandise was second only to that of the Walt Disney Company.

When Roy Rogers officially retired from show business, he had compiled an impressive résumé. He had appeared in more than one hundred motion pictures and had even been inducted into the Country Music Hall of Fame twice, once as a solo artist and once as a member of the group that helped his rise to stardom, the Sons of the Pioneers. Roy even opened the Roy Rogers–Dale Evans Museum in 1967, showcasing all of his and his wife's personal mementos and memorabilia, including a taxidermized Trigger (the museum closed in 2009). Roy Rogers and Dale Evans remained together until Roy passed away on July 6, 1998, less than a year after the couple had celebrated their fiftieth wedding anniversary. Dale died on September 7, 2001, and they are buried beside each other at Sunset Hills Memorial Park in Apple Valley, California. Roy's gravestone bears the signature "Roy Rogers" across the top, with "Leonard Franklin Slye" in print along the bottom.

Back in Ohio, there is a historical plaque and sign erected in front of the Slye house in Duck Run, commemorating the youth of the man who would one day grow to be crowned King of the Cowboys. The property is located alongside Sly Road, which many believe got its name from the Slye family, even though it's missing the *e*. But perhaps appropriately enough, the house itself sits at the intersection of Sly Road and Roy Rogers Road.

PART III
LEGENDARY VILLAINS

KING OF THE BOOTLEGGERS

I think it's fair to say that one does not become the head of a multimillion-dollar bootlegging operation overnight. Then again, George Remus wasn't your ordinary businessman. Sure, he was intelligent and shrewd and always kept a keen eye out for opportunities, but what made Remus unique was that he was always looking to his past experiences to guide him. What's more, he believed that if he studied a situation long enough, he could identify loopholes—loopholes that could be exploited to build his empire. And build it he did, only to have it all come crumbling down when he was betrayed by a member of his own family. This betrayal ended in death, proving that while family can be the ties that bind us together, they've been known to garrote too.

Born on November 13, 1878, in Landsberg, Germany, George Remus immigrated to the United States with his family shortly before his fourth birthday. After several moves, the Remus family settled on Chicago, Illinois, as the place to put down roots in 1885. When George's father, Frank, suddenly fell ill and was unable to work, fourteen-year-old George stepped up and began taking on multiple jobs to help support his family. George would eventually start working at a pharmacy that his uncle owned, and it was there that many thought George found himself a career. He threw himself into his work and appeared to have a genuine love for it, taking on more and more responsibilities until he was essentially running the pharmacy for his uncle. George enrolled in the Chicago College of Pharmacy, excelled in his studies and, after graduation, became a certified pharmacist. When his uncle announced that he was retiring, George went ahead and bought the pharmacy from him, becoming a business owner by the age of twenty-one.

On the home front, Remus married Lillian Klauff on July 20, 1899, and the following year, they welcomed their first child, Romola Remus. Shortly thereafter, George showed just how successful a pharmacist and businessman he had become by purchasing his second pharmacy. To all who knew or did business with him, it was obvious that George Remus had found the secret to success in the pharmacy industry. So, in 1904, when George said he had an announcement to make, most assumed that he had purchased yet another pharmacy. That couldn't be farther from the truth. In fact, George announced that he would be leaving the pharmacy business to become a lawyer. Roughly five years after purchasing his first pharmacy, George Remus was selling it all off to begin a new career in a field that, according to most, he had no experience in.

While the news came to a shock to most, it wasn't entirely true that George had made the leap blindly. In fact, while he was still running his pharmacy businesses, he was also attending the Illinois College of Law. By the time George made the news of his career change public in 1904, he had already graduated and had been admitted to the Illinois bar. Of course, all of that didn't amount to income…yet. First George had to decide what type of lawyer he wanted to be. Attacking the law books with the same vigor as he had his pharmacy reference manuals, George found himself drawn to the idea of having to defend one's actions before a court. He also found that if he looked hard enough, he could find something in the law books that would allow him to justify pretty much anything. For those reasons, George Remus decided that he would specialize in criminal defense. And the harder the case was to defend, the more George wanted it—he began to crave tackling those tough cases, looking at them as something of a challenge that let him dive into his law books to find loopholes.

It was slow going at first, but there was something else going on in Chicago that helped George Remus start to make a name for himself as a criminal defense lawyer: the rise of organized crime. Slowly but surely, "connected" men began showing up at Remus's office, seeking counsel. Remus was always ready to offer his services, especially since these men usually showed up with what appeared to be an endless supply of money. However, the case that would put Remus on the map came in 1914, when William Cheney Ellis came knocking on George's door.

Ellis stood accused of the brutal, premeditated stabbing death of his wife at Chicago's Sherman House Hotel on October 16, 1913. For many, it was an open-and-shut case: Ellis had been found, covered in blood, in the hotel room, along with his wife's body and the murder weapon. But George Remus knew that if he looked deep enough, he'd find a loophole. And he did. In court, Remus stated that while his client did indeed kill his wife, he had no memory of it because it had been committed while Ellis was suffering from "transitory insanity," a condition that could allow a person to commit acts without having any memory of their actions. Remus even went so far as to quote from an obscure book, *The Textbook of Insanity*, by Austro-German psychiatrist Richard Freiherr von Krafft-Ebing, to prove his point.

The fact that this type of defense had rarely been attempted before made the case one of the biggest at the time, and before long, George Remus's name was in newspaper headlines everywhere. Most didn't buy this novel theory Remus was proposing, but it was enough to make the jury reconsider the entire case. On March 6, 1914, the jury reached a compromise: they would convict Ellis of murder but for a reduced sentence of fifteen years, throwing out the idea that the murder was premeditated. Remus's defense had worked, and with that, his career skyrocketed. It is said that over the course of the next five years, Remus's earnings rose to the point that he was pulling in close to $500,000 per year, which would be pushing $6.5 million today.

The year 1920 would represent another turning point in the career of George Remus. It began on January 17, when Prohibition, a nationwide Constitutional ban of alcoholic beverages, went into effect. Across the United States, it was now illegal for anyone to make, sell or even transport alcohol. You couldn't even bring it in from other countries. In short, the United States went "dry." And yet, Remus noticed that many of his mobster clients didn't seem to have a problem acquiring what was now being referred to as bootleg alcohol. In fact, some of them seemed to be making quite a profit buying and selling illegal alcohol. Remus decided that he wanted in on the action, but he needed to find that loophole to protect himself and his profits first. So, he set to work hitting the law books and taking a close look at the National Prohibition Act, also known as the Volstead Act, which officially established Prohibition in the United States.

While he searched for his loophole, George Remus had a new legal issue to contend with: his own divorce. Having caught her husband in an ongoing affair with his secretary, Augusta Imogene Holmes (Imogene to most), Lillian served George with divorce papers. Rather than fight the divorce,

George calmly accepted the terms; almost as soon as the ink was dry on the paperwork, he married Imogene.

It's impossible to pinpoint the exact date George Remus found his loophole, but he discovered it buried in the Volstead Act. On the surface, the Volstead Act made it appear that all alcohol manufacturing and distribution was illegal, which wasn't the case. If a company was distilling alcohol to be used exclusively for medicinal purposes, said company would be considered "bonded" and, as such, would be free to manufacture and distribute that alcohol, legally. And what better person to head up a bonded operation than someone with a pharmacy background like George Remus? Of course, simply manufacturing and shipping medicinal alcohol wasn't going to make George the big bucks, so he came up with another loophole, one that would make him a multimillionaire. He would let some of his former mobster clients and associates know when a shipment was leaving a facility so they could hijack the shipment. That way, they could handle the hard part of moving the now-illegal shipment. On top of that, George could write the entire shipment off as a business loss, which meant he'd be doubling his profits.

It felt like a foolproof plan. There was only one problem: where to set up his distillery from which to run his illegal business. Looking around Chicago, he found that most of the bootlegging was already under control of the various Chicago mobs. George knew better than to cross them or even appear like he was trying to compete for business. George did some research and found that the vast majority of bonded liquor originated from in and around Cincinnati, Ohio. So, guess where the George Remus family picked up and moved to?

It didn't take long for George Remus to be crowned King of the Bootleggers once he got to Cincinnati. Using his pharmacist background, he was able to buy several pharmacies. Many of the Cincinnati-area distilleries had been forced to shut down due to Prohibition, and this allowed Remus to purchase already-established manufacturing facilities for his "bonded" alcohol production. It is said that three years after starting up his business in Cincinnati, George Remus's illegal operation consisted of multiple distilleries (some out in the open, some hidden from sight), a fleet of trucks and close to three thousand employees. George had made himself upward of $40 million.

If there was one thing George Remus liked as much as making money, it was spending it. He became known for throwing extravagant parties at the sprawling estate he and Imogene owned. It was not uncommon for guests to receiving parting gifts of diamond stick pins or brand-new cars. But spending all that money has a way of coming back to haunt you, and George began to wonder if the government might start poking around to see just how he was managing to make all that money so fast. And he knew all too well that if the government found even a fraction of the wrongdoings he was involved in, George could kiss all his millions goodbye, as they would surely be seized. Once again, George looked to his past and began researching laws to see how he could protect his money. What he found seemed to be foolproof: he just had to sign everything over to his wife, Imogene. That way, if the government came calling and tried to seize assets, they could only take what was in George's name, as he was the one doing the illegal activities. They wouldn't be able to touch anything in Imogene's name.

Not long after George had transferred everything over to his wife, federal agents did indeed come calling. It seems the agents decided to take an even closer look at the Volstead Act than Remus had done and found that he was committing all sorts of crimes, eventually charging Remus with thousands of violations of the Volstead Act. As George had surmised, they couldn't touch anything he had put in Imogene's name. And while he pulled out all the stops in his own defense and was able to get most of the violations dismissed or reduced, in January 1924, George Remus was sentenced to two years at the federal prison in Atlanta, Georgia.

Enter Bureau of Investigation agent Franklin L. Dodge Jr. Dodge, who had recently concluded an investigation that resulted in the conviction of a ring of Georgia bootleggers known as the Savannah Four, was working undercover at the Atlanta Federal Prison. While this investigation was designed to look into the alleged misdoings of prison warden Albert Sartain, some say that Dodge felt he could use the opportunity to try and get close to Remus and maybe discover his secrets. Others claim that Remus recognized the agent and had heard Dodge could be bought and might be willing to exchange information for, say, a shorter sentence.

Regardless of how it came to be, Dodge and Remus did indeed meet. As a result, Dodge was able to compile information related to the inner workings of Remus's empire, all of which Dodge turned in to his bosses. What is nowhere to be found in Dodge's documentation was that Remus had let Dodge in on the big secret about how Remus was able to secure his millions by putting it all in his wife's name. But while it was never documented, Dodge's actions made it painfully clear that he was in on Remus's secrets. Shortly after filing his report, Franklin Dodge headed off to Cincinnati to begin a torrid affair with Imogene Remus.

While George Remus sat behind bars, his wife and Franklin Dodge were burning through his money. They took extravagant vacations, went on expensive shopping sprees and liquidated much of the assets that were in Imogene's name, rarely giving any of the proceeds to George. One story has Imogene selling off the entire Fleischmann Distillery for $80,000 and only handing over $100 of the sale to George. Still imprisoned, there was little George could do except bide his time and count the days until his release.

Imogene and Franklin Dodge eventually came to the realization that George Remus was going to be released from prison soon, so they had to figure out a way to get rid of him. They explored solutions as varied as having him deported to even hiring a hit man to murder Remus. But they were quickly running out of time, and as George's release date kept creeping closer, Imogene and Dodge felt they could buy themselves some time by having Imogene file for divorce.

On August 31, 1925, Imogene Remus officially filed for divorce from her husband, George Remus. George was served the divorce papers as he was being released from the Atlanta Penitentiary on September 2, 1925, three months having been shaved off his sentence for good behavior. As if being served divorce papers after stepping outside a free man in almost two years wasn't bad enough, there was a U.S. marshal there, informing George that he would have to answer to additional charges stemming from his original arrest—a misdemeanor charge where George could face up to one year in jail if convicted. Shortly after his release in Atlanta, George Remus was escorted to the local train station and put on a train to Ohio. Last stop: a cell at the Montgomery County Jail.

After a week of being incarcerated, George Remus was able to bond out, using one of the few properties still in his name, the Remus Building in Cincinnati, as collateral. Almost immediately upon posting bond, Remus made his way back to his mansion in Price Hill. Unsure of what awaited him, George found that while most of his staff were still there, his wife, Imogene, was not. When questioned as to her whereabouts, the staff responded that they didn't know, but that she had "gone away" with Franklin Dodge.

While he attempted to get the outstanding misdemeanor charge against him thrown out, George Remus also began to try to minimize the damage his wife and Franklin Dodge had done to his empire. George began by revoking the power of attorney he had given Imogene, transferring it to one of his longtime business associates, Blanche Watson. He hired people to try to hunt down not only his wife and Franklin Dodge but also all of George's assets. George also began filing lawsuits against the pair, both individually

George Remus behind bars. *From the* St. Louis Star and Times, *Saturday, November 19, 1927, original source unknown.*

and collectively, the most famous being one that he filed against the pair on April 2, 1926, seeking $1 million.

On June 7, 1926, the U.S. Supreme Court refused to hear Remus's final appeal, meaning that he was going to have to serve the time. Remus was to surrender to authorities on July 1 and serve his one-year sentence in the Miami County Jail in Troy, Ohio. George Remus spent what little time he had left attempting to find (and hide) as much of his remaining assets as he could. He even tried putting some of his mansion's furnishings into storage, concerned that his wife and Franklin Dodge would loot the property. When the time arrived for George to turn himself in, he was already at the jail, waiting to be taken into custody. He surrendered without incident and began serving his one-year sentence. While incarcerated, he was a model prisoner, and because of this, on March 28, 1927, George was transferred from the Miami County Jail to the Scioto County Jail in Portsmouth, Ohio, putting him closer to home.

At midnight on April 26, 1927, George Remus was once again a free man, and the very first place George wanted to go was home to his Price Hill mansion. Except when he arrived there sometime after 4:00 a.m., what he was looking at was no longer a home. In fact, it was barely a house because it had been stripped almost completely bare. If it wasn't tied down, it was gone. In some cases, even if it was tied down, it was still now missing, right down to the tiles from the indoor swimming pool.

By most accounts, this was what drove George Remus over the edge. Friends said that he would often spend days in the same clothes, wandering around his abandoned mansion, crying. Sometimes, employees would hear him cry out, exclaiming that he could see his wife and Franklin Dodge together. It appeared as if the only thing that kept George Remus going was the thought of revenge. Aside from continuing to fight the divorce and filing suits against both Imogene and Franklin, George also started claiming that Imogene and Franklin were plotting to have him murdered. In response, Imogene and Franklin made statements alleging that George Remus was trying to have *them* killed. The result was that both parties took to having bodyguards with them whenever they were out in public.

It appeared that George might have been on to something when, in the late summer of 1927, a man named Harry Truesdale showed up on Remus's doorstep. Truesdale told Remus that he had been approached back in August and asked if he'd be willing to accept a contract to kill George Remus. He was promised $10,000, which would be given to him in two $5,000 payments from two individuals: Imogene Remus and Franklin Dodge. Truesdale said that he had gone so far as to accept the contract and begin tailing George before getting cold feet and deciding that he couldn't go through with it, instead opting to make George aware of the contract out on his life.

The divorce case of Imogene Remus versus George Remus was finally set to be heard at 9:00 a.m. on October 6, 1927, at the Hamilton County Domestic Relations Court in Cincinnati. The day before, George, who had taken up residence in Cincinnati's Sinton Hotel, had his driver, George Klug, drop him off at his Price Hill mansion for the evening. As he exited the car, Remus told Klug to return tomorrow morning bright and early at 7:00 a.m. and pick him up. Remus said that he wanted to be driven to the Hotel Alms, where Imogene was staying, so he could "talk things over with her" one last time before their final court appearance.

Klug did as he was told, and on the morning of October 6, he was parked outside the Hotel Alms with his boss, George Remus, sitting in the back seat. Before too long, Imogene Remus came out the front door of the hotel and headed for a nearby taxicab. As George watched his wife, he was surprised to see that she was not in the company of Franklin Dodge, but rather Ruth Remus, Imogene's daughter from her first marriage. Once the two women were inside the taxi, George ordered Klug to "get closer" to it. As Klug attempted to pull up next to the taxi, as Ruth would later testify, both she and her mother recognized George Remus, which caused them to tell their driver to "drive fast" to get away.

The taxi driver sped up, attempting to put space between him and George's car. It didn't work, and Klug kept right on the taxi's bumper. In a last-ditch effort to shake the car, the taxi driver made a sudden turn into Eden Park. Still, George Klug stayed right behind them. As the taxi made its way past the park's Mirror Lake, Klug was able to overtake the taxi and swerve in front of it, forcing the taxi driver to come to a screeching halt to avoid an accident. Imogene immediately leapt from the taxi and began running down the road, toward the park's Spring House Gazebo. George Remus sprang from his car and took off after his wife, followed closely behind by Ruth.

George caught up to Imogene right next to the gazebo. Grabbing her by the wrist, George spun her around, pulled a revolver from his pocket and shot her once, point-blank in the stomach. She slumped against her husband, falling to the ground in front of him. As George stared down at his wife, Ruth ran up and grabbed him, screaming, "Do you know what you are doing?" As this was happening, Imogene somehow managed to get back to her feet and began running. Seeing this, George simply pushed Ruth aside and started slowly and methodically walking after Imogene.

Ruth was able to overtake George and began helping her mother toward the long line of cars that had stopped to witness the spectacle. Initially, none of the motorists was willing to help, but one eventually opened his door and he drove the women to the hospital, where Imogene would succumb to her wounds.

After the shooting, George continued down the road toward where he believed George Klug would be waiting with his car. Except Klug, upon hearing the shot, had taken off, leading George Remus stranded. Apparently without a care in the world, Remus walked out of the park and out onto Martin Drive, where a passing motorist stopped and asked if he needed a ride. Remus obliged and asked to be taken to the Pennsylvania Depot nearby. Once at the station, Remus called for a taxi and asked to be taken to the Cincinnati Police Department's Central Station. The taxi arrived at the police station at approximately 8:30 a.m. Remus walked calmly into the station and told the officer at the front desk, "I just shot my wife, and I came to surrender. My name is George Remus." As the officer tried to get more information, Remus is said to have remarked, "This is the first peace I have had in two years and a half."

Obviously, the murder trial of George Remus made national headlines. Even though it appeared to be an open-and-shut case—there were multiple witnesses and Remus himself admitted to the crime—the prosecution was taking no chances and appointed Charles Phelps Taft II, son of former U.S. president and chief justice William Howard Taft, as the lead prosecutor. George Remus decided to represent himself, although he did hire Charles H. Elston to serve as co-council. As for his defense strategy, Remus decided to look to his past once again and dust off a defense he had successfully used back in 1913: transitory insanity.

Throughout the trial, Remus would bring up the activities of Imogene and Franklin Dodge, attempting to show how, over time, Remus was made to suffer until he simply snapped. Remus even called witnesses, including his first wife and members of his Price Hill staff, who testified to seeing Remus's mental state deteriorate as he was made aware of more and more of his wife's activities. The prosecution countered with its own witnesses, most notably Imogene's daughter, Ruth, who painted George as a ruthless, often abusive, man.

When it came time for closing arguments, George Remus delivered the defense's himself. It was an incredibly bold move having someone accused of murder deliver their own closing arguments, especially one who's claiming transitory insanity as a defense. But it worked, as while the trial itself lasted over five weeks, the ten-men, two-women jury needed only nineteen minutes to reach a verdict. On December 20, 1927, they found George Remus not guilty of the murder of his wife, Imogene. George reacted to the verdict by facing the jury and exclaiming, "I wanted American justice and I thank you folks." He was then led from the courtroom while tears streamed down his face. Afterward, one of the jurors, Robert E. Hosford, told the press, "We thought Remus had been greatly wronged, and that persecution had lasted long enough." Hosford also explained that the jury wanted to return a verdict that would have freed Remus entirely, but that the judge did not give them that option. As such, George Remus was sent to the Lima State Hospital for the Criminally Insane for evaluation. Prosecutors continued to argue that Remus was indeed sane and even presented testimony from several well-known psychiatrists. The judge reviewing the case was not swayed though, and Remus was released within a year's time, a free man.

After his release, Remus once again teamed up with Blanche Watson, and they set about trying to recover his lost fortune and, if they found any, re-hiding it because the federal government was still looking for it too. There were rumors that Remus was trying to rebuild his bootlegging empire, but

The legend of the King of the Bootleggers lives on, in bottle form. *Author photo.*

with almost all his assets seized or missing, no collateral and the feds watching his every move, that quickly proved futile.

When Prohibition ended in December 1933, the days of the bootleggers faded into memory. By this time, George Remus had tried his hand at consulting work for Cincinnati lawyers, but the financial benefits of that didn't even begin to come close to the millions Remus had made bootlegging. Thinking that perhaps a change of scenery would do the trick, Remus packed up his Cincinnati belongings and hopped over the Ohio River, settling back down in Covington, Kentucky. Blanche Watson went to Covington with Remus, and they were married in 1941.

George Remus died on January 20, 1952, and was buried at Falmouth, Kentucky's Riverside Cemetery. Despite claims that George spent the rest of his life searching for his missing fortune, hardly any of it was ever located. Or at least, none that was ever made public. Some believe that George was able to find it but was unable to spend any of it for fear that it would attract the attention of federal agents, who continued to pursue Remus until his death. Most, however, are convinced that Imogene Remus spent most of the fortune and then, knowing how determined her husband was, took great care to conceal it where it could never be found.

As for the only other person who might have known the whereabouts of Remus's fortune, Franklin Dodge, it appeared that Imogene hid it from him too. Again, it could be said that Dodge recovered all the missing fortune but dared not do anything with it, but his behavior after Remus's trial seems to contradict that. After Remus's release, Dodge relocated to Michigan, married and began living a quiet, simple life. He started working for the Michigan Liquor Control Commission and stayed there until his retirement. He died on November 26, 1968.

"HE'S DEAD. SHE'S DEAD. THEY'RE DEAD."

Sunday, March 30, 1975. Easter Sunday. Across the city of Hamilton, Ohio, families in their Sunday best were gathering to celebrate with Easter egg hunts and egg roll games. Children would be continually attempting to snatch another handful of jellybeans from their overstuffed Easter baskets without getting busted by their parents for eating too much sugar before dinner. Then, as everyone pushed themselves away from the remains of the ham dinner with all the fixings, time would be spent reflecting on the past bitter cold Ohio winter and longing for the warmer spring weather that was to come. Then, as the last of the Easter sun dipped below the horizon, families would pile into their cars and head home. It was around this time that Hamilton police received a phone call that something horrible had happened on Minor Avenue—something that would forever tarnish Easter Sundays in Hamilton.

The initial call came into police at 9:41 p.m. The caller, an adult male who refused to give his name, said there had been a shooting and gave a Minor Avenue address as the location. The caller then quietly stated, "He's dead. She's dead. They're dead," before hanging up. Police looked up the address and found that it was the home of sixty-five-year-old Charity Ruppert. The name and address didn't ring a bell with authorities, but nonetheless, a patrol car was instructed to drive by and check things out, just to be sure.

When officers arrived at the two-story home on Minor Avenue, nothing seemed to be out of the ordinary. As they approached the house, police found Charity Ruppert's son, forty-year-old James Ruppert, standing in the doorway, just inside the front door. When asked what happened, Ruppert simply stated something to the effect that he had been at the home since 5:00 p.m. Perplexed at Ruppert's response, police looked behind him and initially thought that everything was in order. But then they saw what appeared to be multiple victims lying on the living room floor. Ruppert was immediately detained and backup called for. Then the officers made entry into the home.

A stone's throw from this intersection, something very unpleasant happened on Minor Avenue on Easter 1975. *Author photo.*

No amount of police training could prepare the officers for what they were about to encounter just inside the doorway. Inside, police found the bodies of five children, ages four to seventeen. All had been shot multiple times at close range. Through a doorway at the back of the living room, police entered the kitchen and discovered the bodies of six more adults and children, including the homeowner, Charity Ruppert. Like the others in the living room, everyone in the kitchen had been shot multiple times, save for one individual, who sustained a single fatal gunshot wound to the chest.

"I thought I'd seen everything," Butler County prosecutor John Holcomb would later say after viewing the scene inside the house. "It's absolutely unbelievable."

It was quickly determined that all the deceased were members of Charity Ruppert's family: her son, Leonard Ruppert Jr.; Leonard's wife, Alma; and the couple's eight children. Charity's husband had died many years before, meaning the only member of the Ruppert family to not be murdered that day was Charity's other son, James. Police quickly took James into custody and transported him to the police station for questioning.

The eleven victims were identified as:

- Charity Ruppert, sixty-five
- Leonard Ruppert Jr., forty-two
- Alma Ruppert, thirty-eight
- Leonard Ruppert III, seventeen
- Michael Ruppert, sixteen
- Thomas Ruppert, fifteen
- Carol Ruppert, thirteen
- Ann Ruppert, twelve
- David Ruppert, eleven
- Teresa Ruppert, nine
- John Ruppert, four

Butler County coroner Dr. Garret J. Boone placed all the times of death at 6:00 p.m. Thinking back to James Ruppert's initial statement that he had been at the house since 5:00 p.m. placed him at the scene of the crime. What's more, if James was the murderer, as well as the anonymous male who phoned the crime into police, that meant Ruppert sat alone in the house with the bodies of his family members for more than three hours.

During the initial investigation of the crime scene, police recovered three handguns—two .22-caliber handguns and one .357 Magnum—from the living room. One additional weapon, a rifle, was found leaning against a refrigerator in the kitchen but did not appear to have been fired. More than thirty shell casings were found scattered throughout the first floor of the house. Eerily enough, while such carnage had taken place in such a small house, none of the victims was tied up or restrained in any way. In fact, the only thing out of place that might have hinted at the bloody violence that took place in the house was a single overturned wastepaper basket.

Later Sunday evening at the police station, James Ruppert did give a statement to police, but that was prior to Ruppert's attorneys showing up and telling Ruppert to remain silent. When asked about the content of Ruppert's statement to police, Chief George McNally would only say, "All I can tell you about the statement is that he didn't admit doing it."

The following day, Monday, March 31, Ruppert was arraigned on eleven counts of aggravated murder and bond was set at $200,000. Ruppert did not enter a plea. On Friday, April 4, a preliminary hearing was held, finding sufficient evidence to move forward with trial. On the same day, service was held at Cincinnati's Arlington Memorial Gardens, after which eleven members of the Ruppert family were laid to rest.

The trial of James Ruppert got underway in Hamilton, Ohio, with the case being heard by a three-judge panel. Even without a confession, prosecutors believed that they had enough evidence to get a conviction. Not only was James Ruppert the only one left alive in the house during the murders, but it was his guns that had been used. They also had an officer who had spoken to James Ruppert in person compare Ruppert's voice to that on the anonymous phone call alerting police to the crime. That officer believed they were one and the same and that it was James Ruppert who had called police, from the scene of the crime, and then waited patiently for them to arrive. The three-judge panel quickly reached a verdict: guilty on all eleven counts of murder. Ruppert's crimes would have made him eligible for the death penalty; however, the Supreme Court's decision in *Furman v. the State of Georgia* in 1972 had suspended the death penalty. For this reason, Ruppert was instead sentenced to life in prison.

Even after the verdict, Ruppert's attorneys petitioned the court for a new trial and a change of venue, claiming that there was no way that Ruppert could have received a fair trial since it had been held in Hamilton, where the crime had occurred. They also brought up that the local press had given the case the front-page treatment, even going so far as to declare the incident "The Easter Sunday Massacre." The court agreed, and a new trial was set to begin in June 1975 in Findlay, Ohio, more than 120 miles north of Hamilton.

Easter Reunion Ends In Death For 11 At Hamilton

Not the kind of news Hamilton, Ohio, wanted to wake up to the day after Easter. *From the* Palladium-Item, *Monday, March 31, 1975.*

As Ruppert's second trial began, it quickly became clear that the prosecution hadn't rested since the first trial. Still working without a confession, prosecutors were nonetheless able to produce witnesses who hinted at a possible motive. The prosecution alleged that James Ruppert had become jealous of the success his brother, Leonard, was enjoying. Leonard had a successful career, a wife, a home and eight children—all things James didn't have. In fact, James was the complete opposite. James was forty-one, single, living with his mother and recently unemployed. It was also revealed that Alma Ruppert, Leonard's wife, had dated James before Leonard. Finally, Leonard had recently taken out large insurance policies on himself for his family. Perhaps James thought that if he eliminated the entire family, he would stand to inherit all that money, believed to be more than $300,000.

The prosecution also presented witnesses that testified to the fact that James's mother, Charity, had grown weary of James's drinking and refusal to pay rent. In fact, James told people that his mother was planning to evict him. But the most damning testimony came from individuals who described James's actions in the month leading up to the murders. There was testimony stating that while James was purchasing ammunition for what would become one of the murder weapons, he inquired about how to go about purchasing a silencer for the gun. And then, just a day before the murders, eyewitnesses testified to seeing James Ruppert with his .357 Magnum, shooting at cans along the banks of the Great Miami River in Hamilton. Once again, James Ruppert was found guilty on all eleven counts of murder and once again sentenced to life in prison.

In 1982, James Ruppert's defense attorney, Hugh D. Holbrock, lobbied for a new trial on appeal. This time, Holbrook admitted that his client had indeed pulled the trigger and killed all eleven of his family members, but that he did it because he was insane. Holbrock was so convinced of this that he planned on paying to have expert witnesses flown in to testify to Ruppert's mental state during the shootings. The court granted a new trial, and shortly thereafter, the defense's experts started showing up to testify.

One of the most compelling witnesses for the defense was Dr. Phillip G. Mechanick, professor of clinical psychiatry at the University of Pennsylvania. Mechanick took the stand on June 28, 1982, and spent almost five hours detailing his conversations with James Ruppert and testifying that, in his expert opinion, Ruppert was suffering from "a paranoid-schizophrenia" during the shootings, which "impaired his ability to function in a major way." When questioned as to if Ruppert gave a reason for the shooting, Mechanick testified that Ruppert didn't give a reason or know why he chose to shoot the children. Mechanick remarked that the closest Ruppert came to a confession was when he stated that he believed if there had been more people in the house at the time, he would have shot them too. "I shot every human being in sight," Mechanick testified that Ruppert coldly told him during one of their conversations.

On July 23, 1982, the three-judge panel handed down its verdict, which was a little different than the previous ones. James Ruppert was still found guilty of first-degree murder, but only in the deaths of his mother and brother. He was found not guilty on the remaining nine counts of murder, by reason of insanity. When he was sentenced on July 30, Ruppert was given one life sentence for each of the two convictions, to be served consecutively at the Franklin Medical Center in Columbus, Ohio, a unit of the Ohio Department of Rehabilitation and Correction.

In June 1995, Ruppert was granted a hearing before the state parole board, which denied his release. Release was also denied in April 2015. According to James Ruppert's online inmate file, he is next eligible for parole in April 2025, so his next parole hearing will take place on February 1, 2025, eleven days away from Rupert's ninety-first birthday.

The Easter Sunday Massacre remains the deadliest shooting inside a private residence in U.S. history.

The Murderous Dr. Stees

What does it take to get away with murder? Concocting an airtight alibi? Ensuring there are no witnesses? Leaving no evidence behind? The list is seemingly endless. But in the case of Gene Isaac Stees, all it took was the old college try to pull off the ultimate vanishing act.

Born on January 20, 1932, to Mr. and Mrs. William Stees of Philadelphia, Pennsylvania, Gene Stees had a childhood that appeared boring and normal, at least on the surface. Decades later, allegations of abuse would be slung around an Ohio courtroom, but back then, nothing seemed out of the ordinary.

After high school, Stees enrolled at Grace College in Indiana. This is where he first laid eyes on Helen Taber, who was also attending Grace College. Sparks flew, and the couple were married in 1955. Once again, everything on the surface pointed toward Gene Stees living a quiet life of wedded bliss. He and Helen quickly started a family and had two children, William and Cathy. Helen was enjoying a successful career as a nurse, while Gene continued his studies at Indiana University, where he earned his master's degree and was working on his doctorate. That's when things started to go horribly wrong.

Gene Stees must have had something going on with college campuses. He had met his wife, Helen, on the campus of Grace College, and he would meet Patricia Weathers on the campus of Indiana University. It's unclear exactly when, but at some point Stees and Weathers began having an affair, even though they were both still married to different people.

Despite Gene's attempts to keep the affair hidden, eventually Helen found out, and the couple decided to separate. Helen moved to Ashland, Ohio, and moved in with her parents, Reverend and Mrs. Miles Taber. Gene, having recently landed an assistant professor position at Ohio University in Athens, Ohio, decided to rent a small farmhouse in rural Athens County for himself and his two children. A short time later, Stees moved Patricia Weathers in with him, once again ignoring the fact that both he and Weathers were legally married to other people.

On the morning of Saturday, October 20, 1962, Helen told her parents that she was taking a bus to Columbus, where she was going to meet Gene. From there, they were driving together to Athens, where they would take in the Ohio University Homecoming game. Allegedly, Helen gave hints to her parents that there were hopes of a reconciliation between her and Gene. That's why, initially, Helen's parents weren't too concerned when she didn't return on time. But they became more concerned when Saturday turned into Sunday and they still hadn't heard from Helen. That's when they decided to call the police.

Since Gene Stees was the last person Helen was supposed to have been with, Athens authorities decided to pay a visit to the farmhouse he was renting. Upon arrival on October 23, they were greeted by Gene, who said that his wife was not there because she had gone to visit relatives in Florida. Confused, the police asked Stees why his wife, Helen, would go to Florida, as her relatives lived in Ashland, Ohio. At that point, Stees admitted that the wife he was referring to was actually his girlfriend, Patricia Weathers.

When asked specifically about Helen Stees, Gene denied knowing where she was. Regarding the plans to meet Helen at the Columbus bus station and then attending the Homecoming game, Stees admitted that was true and that he had gone to the Columbus bus station on Saturday, but Helen was nowhere to be found. After waiting and looking for her to no avail, Stees said he turned around and headed back to Athens. When asked which vehicle he drove to Columbus, Stees pointed to his station wagon in front of the farmhouse. An inspection of the station wagon revealed what appeared to be blood, for which Stees had no explanation. Still, the blood was not enough to arrest Stees on a murder charge—or any other charge, for that matter. Police were able to charge him with "living with a woman he falsely represented as his wife" (Patricia Weathers). It wasn't much, but it allowed police to bring Stees to jail while they continued their investigation.

While he was in jail awaiting the resolution of the charge, authorities continued questioning Stees regarding the whereabouts of his estranged wife. Initially, Stees continued to say that he had no idea where Helen was. Finally, on Thursday, October 25, Stees broke down and admitted to killing his wife. He then began to recount exactly what happened on October 20.

As Helen's parents had told authorities, Gene had indeed picked her up at a Columbus bus station, and the pair had driven to Athens with plans on attending Ohio University's Homecoming game later that day. Prior to heading out to the game, Stees drove his estranged wife to the Athens farmhouse he was renting, and at some point, an argument ensued. It was during this argument that Stees admitted hitting Helen in the head with a crowbar while she was standing in the hallway of the farmhouse. He then placed a plastic bag over her head and left her in the hallway. Later that evening, Stees placed the body inside a large steel drum, rolled the drum out to his station wagon and loaded it in. He then drove to Dow Lake, located inside Athens County's Strouds Run State Park, put the drum on a rowboat and made his way out toward the middle of the lake, where he threw the drum overboard.

Once they had Stees's confession, he was immediately charged with first-degree murder. A call was then put out for a dive team to make its way to Dow Lake. That afternoon, under the watchful eyes of some two hundred spectators along the shoreline, a dozen divers searched the bottom of Dow Lake, looking for the steel drum Stees admitted dumping there. Two divers eventually found the drum, sitting in twenty feet of water. When unsealed, the drum was found to contain the remains of Helen Stees. While conducting an autopsy, it was determined that at the time of her death, Helen was pregnant.

Gene Stees's trial began in February 1963. Prosecutor Homer Gail wasted no time in asking the twelve-man jury to find Stees guilty and to pass a sentence of death. Gail contended that Stees had planned the murder of his estranged wife for some time, waiting until his live-in girlfriend was out of town to lure Helen down to Athens to murder her.

Defense attorney Joseph B. Yanity decided not to argue that his client did not commit the murder, but rather that he was "temporarily insane."

BODY IN LAKE

Ohio U. Instructor Admits Slaying Wife

Once authorities recovered Helen's body from the lake, coupled with Stees's confession, his fate was all but sealed. *From the* Times Recorder, *Friday, October 26, 1962.*

As evidence of this, Yanity used Stees's harsh upbringing and put several different psychiatrists on the stand, each claiming that there was evidence to substantiate that Stees was temporarily insane when he killed Helen.

On Friday, February 8, the defense rested, and Judge John Bolin handed the case over to the jury. The judge gave the jury six options for possible verdicts:

- guilty of first-degree murder
- guilty of first-degree murder with mercy recommended
- guilty of second-degree murder
- guilty of manslaughter
- not guilty by reason of insanity
- acquittal

The jury deliberated until 9:30 p.m. Friday evening without reaching a verdict. They were back at it bright and early Saturday morning. At 2:10 p.m. Saturday, the jury announced they had reached a verdict: guilty of first-degree murder with mercy recommended. The jury decided to convict of first-degree murder because they felt Stees's attempt to cover up the crime by hiding the body inside the drum and dumping it in the lake showed premeditation. The "with mercy recommended" essentially meant that the death penalty was taken off the table. Stees would, however, spend the rest of his life in prison. Or so everyone thought.

Gene Isaac Stees officially entered the Ohio Penitentiary in Columbus on February 14, 1963. By all accounts, he became a model inmate and, as a result, was deemed a low-risk inmate, which brought with it certain perks. One of these was that he could be considered for work duty. Stees would eventually transfer to the Records Office, taking a job as a clerk. At the time, inmates working as clerks were permitted to wear civilian clothes instead of the standard-issue striped uniforms. The Records Office was also located at the front of the Ohio Penitentiary, close to the front gate. A perfect storm was

Convicted killer escapes Ohio pen

By the time newspapers started reporting on Stees's escape, he'd already been missing almost five days. *From the* Daily Reporter, *Monday, February 23, 1970.*

building for Gene Stees, culminating on February 18, 1970, when he simply vanished.

No one is sure how Stees managed to pull off his disappearing act, but most believe that since he was in civilian clothes close to the front gate, he simply blended in with the crowd and walked out. Head counts were done in the morning and at night, so if Stees slipped out shortly after the morning count, he would have had several hours' lead time before anyone noticed he was missing. Additionally, the Ohio State Patrol wasn't notified of the escape until almost three days later, more than enough time to get out of Columbus, Ohio, or even the country, if he had the means and support.

For obvious reasons, the first person authorities turned to was Stees's live-in girlfriend, Patricia Weathers. In a strange twist, it was discovered that when Gene was meeting with his estranged wife on that fateful day in 1962, Weathers had gone to Florida to meet with her estranged spouse. Authorities soon learned that while the Stees meeting ended in tragedy, the Weathers meeting led to reconciliation: Patricia Weathers was still happily married and had not heard from Gene Stees since his arrest.

With that, the Gene Stees trail began to grow cold. The Federal Bureau of Investigation (FBI) opened a file on Stees, but after decades without a single lead, it was quietly closed. Today, many believe that even if Stees had survived his initial escape attempt, he is more than likely deceased, as he would be closing in on his ninetieth birthday. However, as of this writing, Gene Isaac Stees, inmate no. 116-595, is still listed on the Ohio Department of Rehabilitation & Corrections' Most Wanted webpage. Individuals with any information related to Gene Stees are asked to contact the Ohio State Highway Patrol at 614-752-2792 or e-mail ohp@dps.state.oh.us.

PART IV
LEGENDARY PLACES

"Whatever You Call Him, It's Still Jesus"

"I'm trying to find a giant statue of Jesus. People say it looks like it's made of butter or cream cheese or something like that."

That was me back in the fall of 2004. I was working on *Weird Ohio* and had just gotten a hot tip on a new roadside oddity from Mark Moran, co-founder of Weird NJ with Mark Sceurman and the ones responsible for all this Weird US business. The problem was this was a new statue, so there wasn't much information to go on, other than that it could be seen from I-75 and was north of Cincinnati, possibly in Lebanon or Monroe. That was all I had at the time, but off I went in search of it.

Looking back, I find it kind of comical that as I was heading south on I-75 that day, every time I pulled off for gas or something to eat, I would ask people if they knew anything about this statue. Most just shrugged, but one cashier just smiled and said, "Keep heading south. You can't miss it. Trust me." I thought he was pulling my leg, but about an hour later, as I continued my journey down I-75 south, something incredibly large came looming up over the horizon to my left. I few U-turns later, there it was right in front of me: a sixty-two-foot-tall sculpture of Jesus—at least his head, arms and torso—apparently rising out of what appeared to be a pond.

The statue, officially named *King of Kings*, was the brainchild of Lawrence Bishop and his wife, Darlene. Back in 1978, the pair had co-founded the Middletown Evangelistic Center in Middletown, Ohio. In the beginning, there were only a handful of members, but those numbers steadily increased; the Bishops took on such a following that in September 1992, they relocated to Lebanon, Ohio, and rebranded themselves the Solid Rock Church. From there, the congregation only continued to grow, as did the campus of the Solid Church. Among other features, there was an outdoor amphitheater with a small pool separating the audience from the stage that would sometimes be used for outdoor baptisms. It was decided that a statue or sculpture was needed behind the amphitheater. Something to face out toward I-75 to maybe attract the attention of passing motorists. Something big—really big. Enter sculptor James Lynch.

James Lynch was handed designs that called for the creation of a sixty-two-foot sculpture, depicting Jesus with his arms raised up toward the heavens. As it was meant to depict Jesus after the resurrection, the Bishops also wanted to include a cross at the bottom of the sculpture. And Jesus was also only to be shown from the torso up, so no legs. No small order, but Lynch set about his work creating the *King of Kings*.

It was decided that the sculpture should consist of a metal frame, over which they would construct a core made of Styrofoam. When it was all sculpted, a thin layer of fiberglass/plastic resin would be placed over the entire piece. The metal frame was created down the street from the Solid Rock Church in Lebanon, Ohio, but since James Lynch was based out of Jacksonville, Florida, that's where the individual pieces that would make up the sculpture were created. Everything was then loaded onto multiple trucks and sent north to Ohio, where all the pieces were assembled over the framework by Mark Mitten. The result was what I was now staring up at from the parking lot of the Solid Rock Church. I grabbed a few photos to use with the story in *Weird Ohio*, hopped back in my car and headed back up I-75. As I passed the *King of Kings* sculpture, I couldn't help but notice the number of skid marks directly in front of the sculpture. Apparently, the new sculpture was already making an impact on motorists.

Fast-forward about a year, and *Weird Ohio*, complete with a story of the *King of Kings* sculpture and a two-page photo, is released…and then all heck broke loose. Its inclusion in the book had suddenly thrown me into the middle of some sort of controversy. Apparently, the sculpture itself had become very polarizing, with people either falling in love with it or seeing it as a bit of overindulgence on the part of the Solid Rock Church. People learning the fact that the sculpture cost $250,000 and was insured for $500,000 didn't help matters. But that wasn't the reason people were e-mailing and texting me. Rather, they wanted me to settle a bet for them: What was the *real* name

The original *King of Kings* sculpture. *Author photo.*

of the sculpture? Easy, right? *King of Kings*. But not so fast, for while the giant sculpture of Jesus was certainly visible to anyone driving up or down I-75, there was no sign saying what it was named. Because of that, motorists started coming up with their own names for it, based on whatever parts of the sculpture stuck out to them.

Most people saw the sculpture's giant arms raised skyward and instantly thought "touchdown," thereby renaming it "Touchdown Jesus." Still others were struck by the slightly off-white color of the entire sculpture, choosing to call it "Cream Cheese Jesus." Comedian/musician Heywood Banks even got in on the action, penning a song about the sculpture, which he called "Big Butter Jesus."

Other than the story appearing in *Weird Ohio*, I'm still not sure why people chose me to settle the debate over the sculpture's name or regale me with their tales and photos of visiting it. But I'm glad they did, and over the years, I have enjoyed hearing and seeing all of it, including the photos of people pretending like they were hi-fiving Jesus or even making his outstretched arms the *H* as groups of family and friends create their "O-H-I-O" photos. Not sure I ever settled the debate, but when cornered, I would admit that I usually referred to the sculpture as "Touchdown Jesus," but I was always quick to add the caveat that "Jesus represents different things to different people, even when he's a sculpture."

We're now in 2010—June 14, to be exact. And my world was about to change forever, on so many levels. My wife, Steph, and I were at the hospital, preparing for the birth of our daughter, Courtney. We had been there since the thirteenth, as the original plan was for Steph to be induced, and we were expecting an uneventful procedure. But because this was our first child and, well, nothing ever goes smoothly at the ol' Willis Homestead, there were complications. Another story for another day, but suffice it to say that as soon as they handed me my daughter and I looked into her eyes for the first time, everything stopped. The next few hours are something of a blur, but once the three of us were back in the hospital room, I can remember texting out and posting a "welcome to the world, Courtney Leigh Willis" message, tossing my phone to the side and lying down to try and get a few minutes' rest. My phone immediately started blowing up, which I thought were just people sending their congratulations, so I turned the phone off so we could get some sleep.

When I finally turned my phone back on, my voicemail was full, and I found myself scrolling through dozens upon dozens of text messages. As I suspected, most were congratulating us, but every single one of the texts and voicemails also mentioning something else: "Touchdown Jesus" had burned down. That's right: at the same time my wife was in labor, the *King of Kings* sculpture was completely engulfed in flames.

When initial reports of the fire hit the Internet, many believed that it was a joke. But it turned out to be true. On June 14, 2010, at approximately 11:00 p.m., the *King of Kings* sculpture was struck by a bolt of lightning, which ignited a flame that quickly engulfed the entire structure. When the flames were finally extinguished, the sculpture was a total loss and there was damage to the Lawrence Bishop Music Theater, the amphitheater the sculpture had stood in front of. All that remained of the sculpture was the scorched metal framework, arms still reaching skyward. It was then that the sculpture was briefly given a new nickname: "Terminator Jesus."

Heywood Banks must have some of the same friends as I do because according to him, his phone was also blowing up with news of his "Big Butter Jesus" burning down. Banks knew what he had to do: write a new verse for his song, which he did. The new lyrics mentioned how the King of Kings had been struck by lightning and even gave the sculpture several new monikers, including "Big Fireball Jesus" and "Extremely Flammable Jesus." While all this is going on, a thread appeared on an online Ohio Conspiracy board that said the combination of "Big Butter Jesus" catching fire while Weird Willis's daughter was being born was a sign. Of what, I was never able to discern, but I'm glad the thread was short-lived and has since disappeared.

While some people took the sculpture's demise as a literal sign from God that it was a "graven image" and should not be rebuilt, Solid Rock Church co-founders and co-pastors Lawrence and Darlene Bishop made it clear that

Farewell, Touchdown Jesus… hello, Terminator Jesus. *Author photo.*

Statue's demise draws big response

The Styrofoam had barely stopped smoking when people started showing up, seeking answers, no matter how far-fetched. *From the* Journal News, *Wednesday, June 16, 2010.*

they were rebuilding. The new sculpture would be different, though, and constructed with nonflammable materials.

Since the Bishops were looking for a new sculpture, they made the decision to go with a different sculptor. They tapped Cincinnati artist and sculptor Tom Tsuchiya, who was responsible for creating the statues of former Cincinnati Reds greats installed outside of Great American Ball Park.

Once a design had been chosen, Tsuchiya created a five-foot clay sculpture from which to work. When it was officially announced that a replacement sculpture had been chosen, the five-foot version was what was shown to the media by Darlene Bishop. This sculpture bore little if any resemblance to *King of Kings* and featured a head-to-toe version of Jesus. His hands were also open wide in a welcoming pose as opposed to reaching toward the sky. The name given to this sculpture was *Come Unto Me.*

Construction on the replacement sculpture began in June 2012. As Tsuchiya was from Ohio, all the work on the sculpture was done locally. Dayton-based Global Manufacturing Solutions worked with shaping and carving the statue in polystyrene, which had a fire retardant in it, just in case. The entire sculpture ended up being fifty-two feet tall, so it needed to be broken into nine separate pieces for shipping to the Solid Rock Church. Before it was broken apart, Display Dynamics from Clayton, Ohio, painted the sculpture to resemble stone. Sadly, Lawrence Bishop would not see this creation brought to life, as he passed away the previous September.

In early September 2012, seven flatbed trucks delivered all nine pieces to Solid Rock Church. Over the course of the next few weeks, the pieces were painstakingly assembled, and on September 19, 2012, all the pieces were finally in place. The sculpture was officially unveiled at a dedication ceremony on September 30, 2012—the one-year anniversary of the death of Solid Rock Church co-founder Lawrence Bishop. At this ceremony, it was announced that the sculpture had a new name: *Lux Mundi*, Latin for "Light of the World." Sculptor Tom Tsuchiya was in attendance, and when he was introduced, he received a standing ovation. The ceremony was capped off by a huge fireworks display, which news outlets remarked were pointed away from the sculpture, just to be on the safe side.

My daughter and I enjoy a flameless visit to the new sculpture. *Courtesy of Stephanie D. Willis.*

Today, I still get questions about the old *King of Kings* sculpture, most of which center on whether I like it better than the new one, *Lux Mundi*. Regarding the new sculpture, people still want me to settle an argument about it: should they call it the "Hug Me Jesus" or the "Five Dollar Footlong Jesus"? And for all you conspiracy theorists out there, please know that my daughter and I have both visited the new sculpture, and neither I nor the sculpture burst into flames.

THE CASTLE THAT SIR HARRY BUILT

When I was but a wee weirdo, I fell in love with castles. Not sandcastles or even the knight-in-shining-armor ones. No, it was the dark, spooky Dracula-type castle for me, complete with a dungeon, of course. I have several distinct memories of my going out into my family's wooded backyard and thinking, "I can build my own castle." Alas, those efforts amounted to nothing more than a few piles of rocks strewn about the trees, which my dad would inevitably knock over whenever he'd decide to stroll around the yard. Talk about crushing a young boy's dreams! So, you can imagine my excitement when, decades later, I moved to Ohio and discovered Harry Andrews, a man who not only had dreams of building his own castle but also spent more than fifty years turning those dreams into a reality that still stands today.

Looking back at the life of Harry Andrews, there's no single "a-ha" moment when he decided that he needed to devote more than half his life to building a castle. Rather, it was a series of events over the course of his lifetime that culminated in Harry deciding to spend his retirement days (and nights) erecting his stone masterpiece. He was born in New York City in April 1890, and the first thing family noticed about Harry was that he was incredibly smart. Harry would often say that he possessed an extremely high IQ and was born with a photographic memory. True or not, it would explain Harry's knack for reading or seeing something and then going out and practically mastering it on his first try. And Harry never needed anyone to tell him to something. Quite the contrary. Harry was a self-starter, to the point that, according to legend, friends would joke that if they wanted Harry to do something, they'd tell Harry that he couldn't do that very thing. That would be all the incentive Harry needed to prove them wrong.

Growing up in New York City, Harry quickly learned to read, and it became something he enjoyed doing. He enjoyed reading the Bible, in particular the Old Testament and stories related to the Ten Commandments. Harry loved the idea that a set of rules and guidelines could be created that also functioned as guiding principles for living one's life. It was also during this time that Harry began to develop a love for ancient architecture, especially Greek and Roman architecture. To Harry, it was amazing that he could see examples of this architecture, some of which was still standing, even though they had been created well over two thousand years ago.

Upon graduating high school, Harry made the decision to continue his studies at Colgate University, a liberal arts college in Hamilton, New York. A large part of Harry's decision was because at Colgate, he would be able to study Greek and Roman architecture. He wasn't sure what he would do with his love of architecture, but he felt as though something was pulling him in that direction. He was still unsure of where his career path was going to take him when he graduated from Colgate University in 1916. But the following year, fate stepped in and led him on the way. It took the form of the United States officially entering World War I. Feeling that it was both a duty and an honor, Harry enlisted in the U.S. Army and was sent overseas to Europe, eventually being stationed in the French city of Toulouse as a medic. It was there that Harry Andrews fell in love with French castles. Working as a medic, Harry worked long, hard hours. Still, Harry managed to spend every spare moment he had roaming the French countryside, marveling at the castles. Much like what drew him to Greek and Roman architecture, Harry was struck by how sturdy these French castles were, apparently impervious to time and the elements. And while it is said that Harry never met a castle he didn't like, far and away his favorite was the Château de la Roche Courbon, which had been built around 1475, atop a site that was believed to have been inhabited since prehistoric times. Talk about standing the test of time!

After World War I ended, Harry made the decision to stay in France under the guise of "studying abroad," even though he was no longer attending any university. He did, however, study Norman architecture at France's Toulouse University for a short period of time.

Harry would eventually return stateside and settled outside Cincinnati. He took jobs as varied as teaching night school, reporting for a local newspaper and working in a mail room. He also began teaching Sunday school classes, where he enjoyed telling his all-boys classes stories from the Old Testament, especially the ones Harry had so loved in his youth. Harry also thought it did a boy well to spend time outside, so before long, he was taking his Sunday school class away on weekend field trips, where they would spend days fishing along the Little Miami River and nights camping under the stars. And while Harry's tales from the Old Testament were fine for during the day, at night, around the campfire, the boys wanted stories much more adventurous. So, Harry began to entertain them with tales of knights and castles from medieval Europe.

Harry would tell the dozen or so boys in his class that, like those who worked to uphold the Ten Commandments, medieval knights also worked within a chivalrous code that worked to restore virtue to society. The boys loved how that sounded, so much so that wanted to become knights themselves! So, one weekend in 1927, as Harry and his group camped alongside the Little Miami River, they all declared themselves part of a new group, the Knights of the Golden Trail.

OK, so they had a name…now what? Well, what were the rules of membership and who could join? Since the group comprised all boys and overnight camping was involved, it was decided that membership would only be open to boys and men. Any boy under the age of eighteen who was accepted into the Knights of the Golden Trail (KOGT) would be referred to as a squire or a page. It was not until a member reached his eighteenth birthday that he could be officially knighted and, from that point on, be addressed as "Sir." As far as the rules governing the KOGT, there was only one: vow to live your life according to what the Ten Commandments said.

Word quickly spread about there being real-life knights camping along the Little Miami River and that they were accepting new members. Before long, KOGT grew to almost one hundred individuals, with a gleeful Sir Harry leading them all. There were problems, though, the biggest being where could all these boys meet? The problem was solved when one of the Harry's students saw that a local newspaper, the *Cincinnati Business Currier*, was running a promotion to grow readership. The promotion stated that anyone who purchased a six-month subscription and paid for it in full would receive the deed for a plot of land along the Little Miami River. The students purchased a subscription, got the deed for the plot of land and promptly sold it to Sir Harry. The KOGT finally had its meeting spot.

Still, there were problems. All the knights had was a plot of land on which they could set up camp. Often, the group would leave the tents and supplies hidden along the property, only to return the following weekend and find it all gone, carted off by wildlife or people who had wandered across the property and discovered the cache. Plus, let's be honest: every good knight needs a castle to defend. So, Sir Harry made his knights a deal. If they would help him drag stones up out of the Little Miami River, Sir Harry would build them their very own castle.

On June 5, 1929, Sir Harry and his Knights of the Golden Trail came together for a small ceremony on the plot of land he had recently purchased. As the group gazed down the hill toward the Little Miami River, they officially laid the cornerstone for Château Laroche—French for "Rock Castle."

Work on the castle began almost immediately, although that sounds a lot faster than it was, as all the work was being done by hand and on the weekends. Sir Harry still had a full-time job too. A typical day of construction would see Sir Harry and the Knights taking empty five-gallons pails down to the edge of the Little Miami River, filling their pails with sandstone rocks from the river, carrying the pails back up to the top of the hill, emptying the pails and then repeating the process over and over. There is some debate as to what exactly Sir Harry was trying to build, at least initially. Most believe that since he was still working full time, that Sir Harry was just trying to create a small, secure structure where he and his Knights could safely store their supplies and camping gear. Others look at what his endeavor turned into and are convinced that Sir Harry's plan all along was to re-create a French castle in Ohio. No official plans for the castle remain (if they ever existed), and Harry is often quoted as saying that while he did have a vague idea of what he wanted to create, he simply ended up building things he thought every castle should have.

As construction continued, Sir Harry and the Knights soon found out that the Little Miami River would naturally provide them with all the sandstone they'd ever need. No matter how many stones they pulled from the river, more would show up every year.

Of course, not everything could be made of stone. To create bricks, Sir Harry came up with the idea of using cardboard milk containers. He would cut the tops of the containers off and fill them with concrete. Once the concrete had hardened, all one had to do was peel the cardboard away and there it was: a brick! Of course, since you had to rip the container to get the brick out, they couldn't be reused, which meant cardboard containers were a hot commodity. In fact, Harry wanted them so badly that if someone stopped by and wanted a tour to see how things were progressing, the tour was free if you had a few empty cardboard milk containers to give. There was something else Sir Harry treated like currency at his castle: rocks. The stranger and more unique the better. Touring the castle today, visitors can see some Sir Harry's favorite rocks, often inscribed with where they came from right on the rock itself.

In 1955, Harry Andrews officially retired from the Standard Publishing Company, telling people that he was now free to work on his castle full time.

The banks of the Little Miami River, with its seemingly endless supply of sandstone. *Author photo*.

Most thought Harry meant he'd treat castle-building as his new full-time job, making a daily commute out to the castle. But what Harry meant was that he had made the decision to move into the castle and live there so that he could work on it full time.

Once he moved in, Sir Harry started working on the castle nonstop. Members of the KOGT would often show up and lend a hand, but Sir Harry threw himself into his work and set himself to the task of furnishing the castle with everything a knight could want. In addition to such boring yet essential rooms like a kitchen, a bathroom and bedrooms, Harry added castle necessities such as a great hall for meetings, a ballroom for dancing, an armory for stockpiling and a dungeon, for imprisoning anyone who dare march against Château Laroche and the Knights of the Golden Trail.

To further protect his castle, Sir Harry built watchtowers and holes along the roof line just in case he needed to drop something down on the heads of unsuspecting foes who were trying to sneak in the front door of the castle. For the castle door, Sir Harry created it using more than 230 pieces of wood, all pieced together in a crisscross pattern to be able to withstand axe blows.

Loveland Castle, with the axe-proof door visible. *Author photo.*

Somehow, even with all the time spent building this castle, Sir Harry still had time to landscape the grounds too. Again, easier said than done, but Sir Harry was going to do whatever his mind thought he could. What made it so hard was that the castle sat atop a hill, which sloped downhill toward the water. No problem, thought Sir Harry, as he just dug up the hillside, creating multi-tiered formal gardens that stretched out more than one hundred feet long. He also created a large vegetable garden with room for twenty-two hot beds.

Over fifty years later, as the world roared into the 1980s. Sir Harry was still working on his castle. Most people thought that the castle, with its multiple stories, was complete. But Harry said there was still work for him to do, even though Sir Harry was now ninety years old. He was working on some additions to the castle so that people "could have weddings up there." When pushed, Sir Harry would say that he was close to completing the castle, maybe 95 percent of the way there. When asked how someone in his nineties was able to continue building a castle with such strength and determination, Harry's response was that he owed it all to the fact that he never smoked, never drank and never got married.

Sir Harry's castle, overlooking the Little Miami River. *Author photo.*

At 10:30 a.m. on Saturday, March 14, 1981, the Loveland Life Squad was dispatched to Château Laroche by a woman visiting the castle. When they arrived, they found Sir Harry, badly burned. According to the woman who phoned, she had just arrived at the castle and was hoping for a tour when she saw a man who appeared to be struggling to put out a fire. The woman then realized that the man's clothes were also on fire. She was able to extinguish the fire but could see that the man had been severely burned, so she called for help.

Sir Harry, in great pain but conscious, said that he was burning some trash when a gust of wind came up, causing the flames to spread outside the burn area. Instinctively, Harry kicked at the flames to stomp them out, forgetting that he was wearing polyester pants, which quickly ignited. Looking over his injuries, it was clear that Sir Harry needed to go to the hospital, but he initially refused, saying that he was fine and had work to do.

Eventually, the medics were able to convince him, and he was brought to the hospital, where Sir Harry was found to have third-degree burns from his thighs to his ankles as well as from his elbows to his hands. His one leg was so badly burned that doctors told him it should be amputated or else the infection could spread through his body and kill him. Sir Harry is said to have refused to have his leg amputated, telling doctors, "You can't build a castle with only one leg." Based on the extent of his other injuries, doctors were still able to admit Sir Harry to the hospital, where they hoped that he would eventually agree to the amputation while they worked on his other injuries. Despite repeated attempts to convince him, Sir Harry held firm: no amputation. On Thursday, April 16, 1981, at the age of ninety-one, Sir Harry Andrews died as a result of infection that had spread through his body.

While Sir Harry kept no official records concerning his bricks and rocks, conservative numbers say that over the fifty-plus years Sir Harry spent working on Château Laroche, he hand made more than forty thousand bricks and made more than fifty thousand round trips up from the Little Miami River with buckets full of sandstone rocks. In his will, Sir Harry gave Château Laroche to the Knights of the Golden Trail, which still maintains it and offers tours. No need to bring any empty cardboard milk containers, but they might be interested in any cool rocks you might have. And please, if you should meet any knights on your tour, please refer to them as "Sir." Sir Harry, if he's still hanging around, would appreciate that.

FINDING UTOPIA IN OHIO

Utopia. A place of perfection. Somewhere where everyone works and lives in harmony with one another. A place where everyone has an equal voice and strives for the better good. Some will tell you that such a place doesn't exist. Even if it did, it certainly wouldn't be in Ohio. But they are wrong. There is a utopia in Ohio. It's just hard to find and even harder to try to live in.

Calling a place "utopia" comes from the idea of a Utopian society—a concept people have been experimenting with and striving toward for hundreds of years, if not longer. But it was French philosopher François Marie Charles Fourier who is credited with giving the lifestyle/philosophy a name: Utopian socialism.

Even after Fourier died in 1837, people were interested in his thoughts as they related to society. Specifically, Fourier believed that most of society's problems were rooted in the fact that not everyone was considered equal. Fourier's solution to all of this, in its simplest form, was to create communities where everyone was equal and shared everything to benefit the greater good of the community. Essentially, it was the idea of communal living—everyone working together for the good of the community as opposed to the good of the individual.

It was some of Fourier's followers who came to southern Ohio in 1844 with the intent of setting up such a self-sufficient society, which they referred to as the Fourier Settlement. Individuals or families who wished to live at the settlement had to be personally invited or else go through an application process to ensure that they were going to agree to the "everyone shares everything" mentality. Once accepted, settlers could purchase a small tract of land and build a home on it, but that property would still be considered owned by the larger community. Likewise, any crops that were going to be grown were for communal use. The community was designed to be not only self-sufficient but also self-governing, with rules and laws being created specifically for the community without any consideration for any other existing laws of the area.

While the idea of a community where everyone is equal and treats one another with respect is a beautiful concept, the harsh reality is that if history has taught us anything, it's that we humans can't function that way. We like our stuff, and by and large, we don't like to share. It didn't take long for community members to start arguing with one another and stop sharing. Soon after, people started leaving, heading back to wherever they had come from in search of the perfect society. All in all, the Fourier Settlement didn't last even three years.

However, the Fourier Settlement didn't remain abandoned for long, and in 1847, John Otis Wattles purchased it with the intent of moving his own group in and rebuilding it. This was not Wattles's first foray into creating a Fourier-type community in Ohio. In 1844, he founded the Prairie Home Community, although that lasted a mere six months before folding. Still, Wattles purchased the entire Fourier Settlement because he felt that this time, he could make it work, especially since Wattles's community would also be based on something else that was sweeping across the world at the time: Spiritualism, the belief that ghosts and spirits existed and could communicate with the living.

When Wattles and his followers moved in, they immediately gave themselves a collective name: The Excelsior. One of the first things they did was to erect a two-story brick building at the far end of the property, right along the shore of the Ohio River. The combination of this group being isolated as well as involved with Spiritualism has shrouded the historical records concerning this building. The building is, in various documents, referred to as a "meeting house," a "dance hall," a "dining hall" and "sleeping quarters." But the strangest point of contention is how and why the building was constructed. According to legend, the brick building already existed on the property, but while communicating with the spirits, Wattles and his followers were instructed to disassemble the building brick by brick, haul it down to the Ohio River and rebuild it exactly as it once was.

Regardless of how and why the two-story brick building along the Ohio River came to be, by December 1847, it was complete. On the evening of December 13, 1847 (again, the historical records disagree on the date: a historical marker at the site gives the date as December 13, while local newspapers reporting on the event at the time have the date as December 15), heavy rains caused the Ohio River to overflow its banks, flooding the entire first floor of the brick building. At about 10:00 p.m., thirty-two people who had "taken refuge from the flood in the great new brick building" saw that the floodwaters were now invading the second floor, where they were currently situated. They then heard a sickening noise that meant only one thing: the building was starting to collapse due to the new mortar not being fully set and able to withstand the river water flowing over it.

When the first wall of the building fell, it trapped several people, pinning them down under the water. Seeing this, some of the people inside decided that it was better to take their chances with the freezing-cold floodwaters than to risk being crushed under the falling walls. So, they jumped into the dark water. All who did were almost immediately swept away by the current. The remaining walls collapsed shortly after that.

It is estimated that from start to finish, it took the Ohio River floodwaters less than five minutes to demolish and wash away almost any trace of that brick building. During that time, seventeen people—more than half of those inside the building at the time—lost their lives. John Wattles survived, but to say he and the remaining members of Excelsior were devastated by the tragedy would be an understatement. The community was once again abandoned, this time without having been in operation for even an entire year.

The final person to take a shot at creating a lasting utopia in Ohio was Josiah Warren. He arrived with his associates shortly after the December flood tragedy and set about trying to rebuild. Although Warren certainly

Heart-rending Calamity!!
FALL OF A BUILDING—SEVENTEEN LIVES LOST!!!

One of the first, and only, newspaper accounts of the tragedy. *From the* Portage Sentinel, *Wednesday, December 29, 1947.*

held onto certain Utopian beliefs—in fact, he is often credited with officially naming the community Utopia—he also had somewhat radical views regarding how to govern. Essentially, he didn't want any sort of organized government; the quote most often attributed to him states that he wanted "no organization, no indefinite delegated powers, no Constitutions, no laws." For this reason, some refer to Warren as one of the first American anarchists.

Even though Warren left the community after just a year, he had laid the groundwork for what he believed would allow everyone to thrive and the community to grow. As in the past, people wishing to settle here had to be given a personal invitation, and everyone within the community were to ensure that they functioned as their own independent entity. In the beginning, it seemed to be working, and more and more people, including families, wanted to join the community. As a result, construction continued, quickly surpassing the number of buildings at either of the other previous communities. At the community's high point in the 1850s, there were close to forty buildings standing, including homes and businesses.

But with growth came problems. For one, the community had grown to the point where they were butting up against neighboring villages. When the community approached some of the villagers with offers to buy their property, they found many of them were not too keen about becoming part of a self-governed community and refused to sell. The price of available land had also gone up exponentially, further impeding expansion. There were just too many people and not enough room to grow, so it began to get crowded and people started leaving for more wide-open spaces. So many left that the community dropped the "invite only" rule to allow anyone who wanted to move in. It didn't help, and by the 1870s, while a few of the original members of the community remained, Utopia had become a literal ghost town.

In 2003, the Ohio Bicentennial Commission erected a historical marker along the OH-52, the Ohio River Scenic Byway, marking the approximate location of Utopia. There are also usually green road markers to let you know when you've officially entered Utopia. Unfortunately, those signs often have a habit of disappearing, much like Utopia itself.

CONNECTING THE DOTS IN ATHENS

Did you know that Athens, Ohio, is the thirteenth-most haunted location in the world? It's true, the British Psychical Society said so! Know what makes it so haunted? It's the fact that if you connect five of the most haunted cemeteries surrounding Athens on a map, they form the shape of a pentagram. Really! I read all about it on the Internet!

I was first exposed to the legend of the Athens Pentagram shortly after I relocated to Ohio in 1999. I was already aware of Athens's Ohio University's reputation as the "Halloween Party School," as well as Spiritualist Jonathan Koons's work in the area in the 1800s (more on him later), but I had never actually visited Athens before. Upon my first visit, I was struck by the underlying spooky vibe that seemed to permeate the area and began to wonder if perhaps there was something to this Athens Pentagram legend. I decided to see if I could find actual evidence of this pentagram. On paper, it seemed like an easy enough thing to do: conduct a little research to get the names of the five cemeteries, track down all five to ensure they exist, draw them up on a map and see what takes shape, literally. Sounds easy, right? But that was more than twenty-three years ago, and I'm still searching for answers. Heck, I even happened to befriend a cartographer who had tried to track down the cemeteries, and even he's still looking for answers (more on him later too).

What makes the Athens Pentagram legend so fascinating, and frustrating, is that almost every single aspect of the tale has changed over time, right down to which cemeteries are involved. Case in point, the following is an alphabetized list of all the cemeteries that have been named as one of the "points" of the Athens Pentagram:

- Basset
- Cuckler
- Gilham
- Haines
- Haning/Hanning
- Higgins
- Hocking
- Hunter
- Littler
- Mansfield
- Matheny/Methany
- Mt. Cole
- Peach Ridge
- Pruden
- Simms

- Snowdon
- West State Street
- Zion

Further complicating things is that, over time, some non-cemeteries have entered the mix as "points" on the Pentagram, most notably Mount Nebo and Ohio University's Wilson Hall. If that weren't enough, there's some confusion as to if it's really a pentagram at all. Some believe that the shape is actually a pentacle, which is essentially a pentagram inside of a circle. Those who believe that the shape is a pentacle will tell you that there are *twelve* locations that make up the shape—five for the pentagram, with the remaining seven forming the circle around the pentagram.

I figured that the best place to start my research would be with the British Psychical Society. Clearly, if it deemed Athens the thirteenth-most haunted place in the world, the Pentagram would have played a major role in that declaration. There was only one problem: the British Psychical Society doesn't exist. There is, however, a Society for Psychical Research (SPR), sometimes called the British Society for Psychical Research. Founded in 1882, SPR was created "to examine claims of psychics and paranormal phenomena," meaning it's more interested in proving or disproving specific claims rather than declaring a location "haunted." In other words, it's highly unlikely that the SPR would have created any sort of "most haunted" list. Indeed, e-mail communications I have had with SPR over the years confirm that it has nothing in its records related to the Athens Pentagram. With that, I realized that I'd have to hit up the ol' microfiche and start digging through the archives to see when people first started talking about the Athens Pentagram.

While it doesn't mention the Pentagram or ghosts, a 1956 article from the *Athens Messenger* contains enough elements of the legend that it should be considered as a contributor to the tale. The article concerns "13 small rural cemeteries" clustered together in one small location in Athens. While the article takes a historical approach, it does mention that the number of cemeteries "in such a small area is unusual." What's more, several of the cemeteries that would become part of the Athens Pentagram legend are discussed in the article, most notably Simms, Matheny and Haning.

The earliest printed account I could find related to the Athens Pentagram was a Sunday, October 26, 1969 article in the *Athens Messenger*. While written very tongue-in-cheek, it nonetheless refers to the British Metaphysical Society ranking "one Peach Ridge grave spot as the 13th most haunted cemetery in the world." The author also comments, almost as an aside, that Haines Cemetery is haunted by the "insanity of a Civil War officer who committed dastardly deeds and destroyed his family homestead near the graveyard." While I'm not sure how an "insanity" is able to haunt, the fact that the statement was included in this article would be the reason why, just a few years later, Haines Cemetery would become known as one of the points of the Athens Pentagram.

Likewise, an article in the Sunday, August 28, 1977 edition of the *Athens Messenger* makes no mention of a pentagram but does say that Athens is "supposedly one of the most haunted places on Earth." The article also states that "curious students still travel up to the 'haunted' Peach Ridge and Simms Cemeteries looking for a good scare."

By October 1977, the Pentagram had begun to take shape, even if all the names of the cemeteries weren't being made public just yet. On Thursday, October 27, the *Athens Messenger* featured an article claiming that "there are 5 cemeteries in the Peach Ridge area" and that "if the five cemeteries are plotted on a map, they form a pentagram, a witchcraft symbol to both focus magical powers and to defend against evil spirits." It also adds that "it is generally believed that two of the cemeteries—Simms and Haning—are haunted." The October 27 article adds several key elements to the Athens Pentagram legend: there are five cemeteries, all in the Peach Ridge area, that form the shape of a pentagram. What's more, it also provides a reason why the Pentagram was created: to focus magical powers and for protection. Finally, we are given the names of two specific cemeteries, along with the statement that they are the only two of the five that are said to be haunted.

So, was there something in the ghost lore of either Simms or Haning Cemetery that would explain why they were part of a pentagram? Not really, other than the fact that in the case of both, they have long-standing ghost stories associated with them. Before joining the Pentagram, Haning Cemetery (often spelled "Hanning") was a popular late-night hangout for area teens and was said to be a place where "séances would take place." Some of these séances were alleged to have had strange results, including one in 1969 "when the heavily padlocked gate of the cemetery unlocked and opened on its own" and another in 1970 when the spirit of a deceased Ohio University student was supposedly contacted by a group of his friends. Haning Cemetery was also rumored to be home to "the ghost of an old man in a long robe."

As for Simms Cemetery, this was probably the most well known of all the area haunts in the '60s and '70s, most likely due to it being a small, out-of-the-way cemetery where, once again, local teens would gather to do teenager things. So, of course, Simms had to be haunted. Most of the ghost stories involved family patriarch John Simms, described as the "local hangman" who would often take to hanging people from a tree in his own backyard, conveniently located near his family cemetery. The tree was still there, and if one got close enough, they'd see there were still rope marks on the tree. Sometimes people would even see ghosts hanging from the tree, or worse, they'd encounter the spirit of hangman John Simms himself. This ghost story continues to this day, even though the 1850 and 1860 census records list John Simms's occupation as "farmer."

As the 1970s were coming to an end, four of the five points of the Athens Pentagram had been confirmed…maybe. Along with Simms and Haning, Haines had officially joined the mix, along with Peach Ridge, which may or may not have been the name of the actual cemetery. Some believe that the news articles were referring to an unnamed cemetery on Peach Ridge. Regardless, the Pentagram was short one point, leaving inquisitive investigators to simply choose a cemetery on their own—preferably one that helped draw a nicer pentagram on a map. Not to worry if you couldn't find one on your own because something magical happened that would make plotting things out a lot easier: the Pentagram became a Pentacle.

That's right, the legend mutated to the point where the Pentagram was now within a giant circle, meaning there were now twelve cemeteries involved—five for the Pentagram itself (Simms, Haines, Snowdon, Cuckler and Mansfield) and seven for the surrounding circle (Hocking, Littler, Gilham, Basset, Mount Cole, Pruden and Hunter). If you're keeping score at home, you'll notice that one of the original "points," Haning Cemetery, had fallen off the list. Not to worry—it will be back before long.

The 1980s became something of a mix-and-match decade for the Athens Pentagram in that people would arbitrarily pick five cemeteries and claim that they were the ones that made up the shape. In some instances, the Pentagram stayed a pentagram (in other words, with no circle around it), meaning only five cemeteries were needed with twelve to choose from. The result was that there were all sorts of variations of the Athens Pentagram's five cemeteries, most created without ever consulting a map to see what shape was formed by connecting the cemeteries.

The 1980s was also the time when the notion that all the cemeteries were haunted, as opposed to just a few of them, became popular. For this reason, new Athens-area cemeteries started to get pulled into the Athens Pentagram legend simply because they were known as being haunted.

The "haunted" angel at West State Street Cemetery. *Author photo.*

Didn't seem to matter that they were nowhere near the Peach Ridge area. Case in point: A popular ghost story surrounding a cemetery in Athens was one related to the West State Street Cemetery. Sitting just inside the West State Street entrance was a tall statue of an angel—a monument to honor the unknown dead in the cemetery. It is said that late at night, the statue would come to life and flap her wings, whisper to people as they walked by and sometimes even cry.

One final change to the Pentagram legend that began to take place in the '80s was the resurrection of the "most haunted" line. Having lain dormant for a time, by the time "most haunted" returned, several key components had changed. For one, it was no longer a specific gravestone or even a cemetery that was the most haunted in the world—it was *all* of Athens. The group that had declared Athens the thirteenth most haunted had changed, too, and the claim was now attributed to the Society for Psychical Research—the real organization. This is the result of the first non-cemetery location being added to the list of "points" in the Athens Pentagram: the mysterious Mount Nebo.

At first glance, it might be confusing as to why a location became part of what was traditionally an all-cemetery legend. But Mount Nebo and what took place near it have a major impact on the stories associated with the area. All because of a man named Jonathan Koons.

Koons was an Athens County farmer who, in 1852, claimed to have received messages from spirits. These spirits provided specific instructions on how to create a Spirit Room that would facilitate communication between humans and the spirit world. Koons and his family spent more than six months building the Spirit Room near Mount Nebo and opened it to the public in 1853. Visitors to the Spirit Room were treated to séances during which ghosts were said to not only make appearances but also speak and, in some cases, play instruments in what can only be described as a ghostly jam session. For obvious reasons, the Spirit Room was a huge success, and for the next few years, people came from all over the United States (and even from overseas) just to visit. During the time the Spirit Room was in operation (1853–58), some began to refer to Athens, Ohio, as a very "spiritually active" area, due mainly to Koons and his séances, which had grown so popular that Koons's neighbors even started building their own versions of the Spirit Room. Of course, calling a place "spiritually active" in these modern times might cause confusion as to what exactly one is talking about, so perhaps the term got replaced by the spookier "most haunted."

Okay, back to the Pentagram. So now we're into the 1990s, and this is where the biggest non-cemetery location starts popping up in the Pentagram legend: Ohio University's Wilson Hall. But not content with just being a point, Wilson Hall becomes the literal center of the Pentagram.

Wilson Hall has long been rumored to have been haunted, with some going to far as to say that Wilson Hall was the most haunted location on campus. The original ghost stories associated with Wilson Hall had no apparent connection to the Athens Pentagram. In fact, they revolved around a specific room on the top floor where something most foul (and bloody) took place, resulting in the face of the devil appearing in the wood grain of the door for some reason.

The first printed record I've found connecting Wilson Hall to the Athens Pentagram is an article in the October 31, 1991 issue of *The Post*, which states, "Wilson Hall is in the center of an imaginary pentagram formed by the many gravesites surrounding this area." I struggled with that sentence. "Imaginary" as in "doesn't exist" or just that you can't see actual lines drawn in the earth? And by saying "many gravesites," is the author implying that there are more than five points involved? The article then goes on to take several components of the Pentagram legend and mash them together. See how many errors you can spot: "The county's Peach Ridge Road sports five graveyards, many believed to be haunted by spirits. Hanning Cemetery has been called the 'thirteenth most haunted place in the country.' In 1970, Simms Cemetery was the site of a séance that supposedly contacted an OU student who had recently died."

But not everything in the article is bad, as it's one of the first printed records I could find that attempts to explain why Wilson Hall is in the center of the Pentagram and why the hall is so haunted: "Legend has it that a separate cemetery was created to keep the spirits of 'bad' people from coming into contact with the 'good' people buried in the other cemeteries. This graveyard was located within the pentagram to focus on mystical energies against evil ghosts—the same place on which Wilson Hall now stands."

It's now the early 2000s, and here come the paranormal reality TV shows. While none of the shows attempted to tackle the legend of the Athens Pentagram head-on, it was touched on in several, none more prominently than *Scariest Places on Earth*.

As noted, the segment from the show is more about Athens, Ohio, than the Pentagram legend. It does, however, open the segment with this statement: "According to the British Society for Psychical Research, the thirteenth most haunted place on earth is Athens, Ohio." Where the Pentagram legend really comes into play is in the quick-cut visuals that serve as transitions throughout the segment. During these transitions, the image of a pentagram shape is clearly shown on a map, along with quick cuts of some of the names of the points of the pentagram. The points shown are Mount Nebo as the top point, Mansfield Cemetery on the right, Cuckler Cemetery on bottom right and Snowdon Cemetery on the bottom left. The far left point is always obscured and is never revealed.

The door to Wilson Hall's infamous room, said to be chock full of paranormal happenings. *Author photo.*

The final part of the Athens segment includes a young man serving as a tour guide of Wilson Hall to a small group of what appear to be students. While he does not mention the pentagram, the tour guide does make several references to elements of the legend, including the erroneous claim regarding Wilson Hall that "a student on the fourth floor committed suicide and under strange circumstances. And ever since then, it has really held the reputation as the most haunted location on campus." Finally, in a perfect example of early paranormal TV shows' credo of "give the people what they want," the tour guide, while standing outside Wilson Hall at night, has his tour group bend down and touch the grass, proclaiming, "The ground you are feeling right now is Indian burial ground—sacred ground to Native Americans. So, this has been holy grave site for centuries."

Okay, so now we're at the point of the timeline where I first got involved. It's the early 2000s, and I'm determined to get to the bottom of the Athens Pentagram legend. I can still remember that when I first dove into the legend, I was stuck by how many cemeteries Athens County has. Hundreds of them. Most are small, family-type cemeteries consisting of only a few stones. Looking at them all on a map, it's easy to see that you could connect cemeteries to form any type of shape you desired. Truth be told, staring at an Athens County map for far too long one day was what gave rise to my proclaiming that Ohio University's Peden Stadium was surrounded by the Athens Rhombus. But what about those cemeteries? Was there something lurking inside them that would prove they were part of something bigger? Enter cartographer and friend Jeff Craig.

I first met Jeff back in the early 2000s, when he applied to join my then-fledgling paranormal research group, The Ghosts of Ohio. Over the years, Jeff and I have had many strange and spooky adventures together, including spending the night inside haunted prisons, crawling through abandoned tunnels and even searching the TNT area in search of Mothman. But it was when Jeff asked to pick my brain (and raid my personal library) on information about haunted places in Ohio that I learned that Jeff was a cartographer and was planning to create a map, titled *Hidden Ohio*. Recently, when I asked Jeff how he first got involved with the Athens Pentagram, he tried to blame me. And while I certainly might have been partially responsible, it was Jeff's drive and lifelong love of maps—as well as, as he put it, "to know what was at the edge of the maps, or beyond"—that really made him want to take the Athens Pentagram legend to the next level: Jeff was planning on tracking down and visiting the five cemeteries that, at least in 2005, were the points of the Pentagram: Simms, Mansfield, Zion, McCole and Higgins.

Jeff planned for his trip by breaking out USGS maps and locating the five cemeteries. Then he gassed up and took off in search of them. Jeff said that, first and foremost, he wanted to see if the cemeteries actually existed. But more than that, he wanted to know what they looked like. Were they spooky-looking? Would he get any weird feelings while he was walking the grounds? Any signs that would somehow reveal that these cemeteries were special or part of something bigger…like a pentagram?

As luck would have it, Jeff visited Athens during an ice storm, which prevented him from visiting all five cemeteries. He still jokes that maybe "unseen forces" were trying to keep him from the cemeteries, but I'll leave that up to my readers to decide. For the cemeteries that Jeff was able to visit—Mansfield, Zion and McCole—there was nothing strange about them at all. Mansfield and McCole were small family cemeteries, while Zion appeared to be a "standard country church cemetery."

Cartographer Jeff Craig's rendition of the Athens Pentagram. *Courtesy of Jeff Craig / celticmaps.com.*

So now comes the $1 million question. I asked Jeff whether, in his professional opinion as a cartographer, he believed the Athens Pentagram was intentionally created. His answer was short and to the point: "I do not think it's intentional. It's a coincidence—a remarkable concurrence of circumstances." I would have to agree. The idea of someone physically laying out five to twelve locations so that they form a specific shape with another location sitting in the middle of said shape is improbable, if not impossible. Yet the legend persists. What's more, over the years, the legend of the Athens Pentagram picks up bits and pieces of other area legends, pulling them in and re-creating them, breathing new life into ghost stories that might otherwise been lost to time. This proves, at least to me, that all good ghost stories never die—they just mutate every four to five years.

PART V
THE UNEXPLAINED

HOPPING AFTER THE LOVELAND FROG

When I first moved to Ohio back in 1999, I immediately noticed something: Ohio is a weird state. What's more, it is proud of its weirdness. So, it would stand to reason that Ohioans would do everything possible to stand out whenever weirdly possible, even when it came to their cryptids. So, if there was a cryptid that was known internationally, Ohio had to have its own homegrown version. Bigfoot? How about the Ohio Grassman? Loch Ness Monster? Well, be sure to visit Lake Erie and check out South Bay Bessie. But Ohioans weren't content to just have their own version of world-famous cryptids. Instead, they wanted some that no other place in the world could claim to have. With that in mind, allow me to introduce you to the Loveland Frog, a four- to five-foot-tall half-man, half-frog creature said to be stalking the waters around Loveland, Ohio, since 1955.

Officially, the first person to have encountered the Loveland Frog was Loveland patrolman Ray Shockey. According to legend, Shockey was traveling along Kemper Road near the Little Miami River when came across what he thought was a small dog lying dead in the road. As Shockey got out of his car to attempt and move the dog from the road, a large froglike creature stood up on two legs and ran toward the guardrail. Some accounts have Shockey firing at the creature as it hopped over the guardrail, down the embankment and into the Little Miami River. The date usually given for Shockey's encounter is March 3, 1972. The only official account of

In Loveland
Frog'll boggle minds

Headline from the *Journal Herald* article that first introduced Ohio to the creature that would become known as the Loveland Frog. *From the* Journal Herald, *Wednesday, April 12, 1972.*

Shockey's encounter appeared in the April 12, 1972 edition of the *Journal Herald*, which stated that "Shockey only told his immediate supervisors about it for fear of arousing alarm among area residents."

The *Journal Herald* article also goes into detail about the very next sighting of the Loveland Frog, again involving a Loveland patrolman. "A week" after Shockey's encounter, his partner, patrolman Mark Matthews, "was walking along the same spot on Kemper Road" when he saw the creature for himself. Matthews, who is quoted many times in the *Journal Herald* article, describes what he saw as a "thing about three feet long and with a face like a frog." Matthews said he "wanted to see what it was," and to do that, he decided to unholster his .357 Magnum service revolver and fire. He alleges to have "hit it four times," after which the creature "gave one last hop" and fell into the Little Miami River, where it disappeared.

It's interesting to note that Matthews's encounter is almost identical to the story regarding Shockey's meeting with the Loveland Frog, right down to the officer firing at the creature while it attempted to escape by jumping the guardrail and heading down toward the water. Another interesting aspect of the *Journal Herald* article is how Matthews himself describes his encounter, as his story will change in the coming years, including his claim that he shot and killed the creature, identified it as an iguana and put it in his trunk to show everyone back at the police station. Matthews doesn't mention any of that in the *Journal Herald* article. In fact, the article goes on to say that to aid in possibly identifying the creature, a composite sketch was made based on descriptions by both Matthews and Shockey. When completed, the sketch was sent to Perry Wakeman, a zoologist at the Cincinnati Zoo, who could not identify what it was. Wakeman said he did not believe that it could have been a giant frog, for while they do exist, they are nowhere near the size of the creature Matthews and Shockey reported seeing. They would also certainly not be able to survive in Ohio's March climate.

All of that did little to put down stories of the Loveland Frog. In fact, the legend grew, quite literally, over time. Some current online versions of the story now put the Loveland Frog at upward of four to five feet and standing erect on two webbed feet! But in terms of actual confirmed sightings, those were few and far between. In fact, several decades would go by until someone would step forward, video in hand, to claim that they had come face to face with the Loveland Frog.

Sam Jacobs reported that on the evening of Wednesday, August 3, 2016, he and his girlfriend were playing *Pokémon Go* near Loveland Madeira Road, close to Lake Isabella, when they saw what Jacobs described as a "huge frog near the water." He was able to grab a few photos and a video before "the thing stood up and walked on its hind legs." Jacobs went so far as to provide a local TV news station a video of the creature.

Unfortunately, the video did little to convince people that Jacobs had indeed seen the Loveland Frog. The video is incredibly dark, which only serves to bring out the most suspect part of the clip: the creature's eyes. In the video, the eyes of the creature are incredibly bright, to the point that it's clear they are giving off their own light, as opposed to any type of eye shine caused when bright lights reflect off an animal's eyes. This is further evidenced when, at the end of the video clip, the creature appears to turn away from the camera, yet both eyes continue to give off the same amount of light. Finally, there is the fact that I was personally able to re-create Jacobs's Loveland Frog using a frog-shaped solar yard ornament my wife found for me on clearance at a local Big Lots store. Granted, it's not exact, but the solar eyes of my frog are close enough to call the authenticity of Jacobs's sighting into question.

However, Jacobs's alleged sighting brought the Loveland Frog legend back to the forefront. On top of that, one local reporter was able to track down Patrolman Matthews, now retired and living in Florida, asking for a comment on the latest sighting. And while Matthews may have wanted to end all this Loveland Frog business once and for all, his comments to the reporter only deepened the mystery.

Matthews told the reporter that what he shot that night in 1972 was "a large iguana about 3 or 3.5 feet long." Matthews also said that he didn't immediately recognize what it was since the iguana was missing its tail. But perhaps the strangest statement Matthews made was that he not only shot the creature but also killed it and was able to recover the body because it didn't, as he first reported, fall into the Little Miami River. In fact, Matthews put the body in the trunk of his cruiser and took it to Patrolman Ray Shockey, who, according to Matthews, said it was the same creature he had seen.

The day the Loveland Frog showed up on my doorstep. *Author photo.*

So, this is where things start to get weird, for while Matthews was obviously attempting to clear up what really happened in 1972, he ended up contradicting the initial reports. Specifically, he changed his initial statements about the creature hopping away to now killing it, placing it in the trunk of his car and bringing it to Shockey so that he could identify it too. If we are to believe that's what happened, then why was time spent creating a sketch to send to the Cincinnati Zoo if the creature had already been identified and Matthews had the animal's body in his trunk? So many questions. Unfortunately, during that interview, Matthews said that he was done talking about the Loveland Frog, so perhaps we'll never have the answers.

But wait, what about the alleged sighting of 1955? Well, I've saved that for last because that's when things get truly bizarre. For while 1955 is usually listed as the year the Loveland Frog was first sighted, that creature was most definitely not the same one Shockey and Matthews saw in 1972. Not even close.

When it comes to the 1955 sighting, most websites and even a few books retell the same vague story, centering on a "businessman who wishes to remain anonymous" driving home late one night. As he winds his way along the Little Miami River, he spots several objects, which he initially mistakes for men, standing on the side of the road (in some versions, the objects are hiding under a bridge). As his car gets closer, the businessman realizes that the objects aren't human at all. Instead, what he sees are three creatures, which are usually described as standing on two webbed feet, between three to four feet tall, with leathery skin and froglike heads. In other words, Frogmen.

Initially, I was willing to dismiss the 1955 sighting altogether since much of what is out there reeks of urban legend, right down to the witness not being named. After much digging, I was able to find copies of notes from individuals who interviewed this mysterious businessman, where he described exactly what happened that night in 1955. Reading through these notes, which also include sketches of what the creatures looked like, it's clear that these are not the same type of creature that was seen in Loveland in 1972, although history and the Internet have forever joined the two events. Of course, it also raises the question as to who or what was lurking alongside that road in 1955. But before we attempt to answer that question, we first need to look at another strange event that took place in 1955, this time in Kentucky.

On the evening of August 21, 1955, two carloads of adults and children came roaring up to the Hopkinsville, Kentucky police station. The men who jumped out of the vehicles and rushed inside the police station were extended members of Sutton family, and they had quite the story to tell. According to them, they needed police assistance because their rural farmhouse had been under attack for the last several hours by creatures from another world. Shortly after one family member reported seeing a strange light come down from the sky, their house was attacked by upward of a dozen creatures, all of which were roughly three feet tall with oversized heads, arms that extended almost to the ground and large eyes that seemed to give off a yellowish light. Their bodies gave off a silvery shimmer, leading the family to believe that the creatures were wearing some sort of silver spacesuit. If they were suits, they were certainly strong, as the creatures seemed impervious to bullets fired at them by Sutton family members. When fired upon, a sound was heard "like hitting a metal bucket," meaning the bullets were hitting something. But the creatures would just jump backward and scamper off, only to return a short time later.

While skeptical, the police agreed to follow the Sutton family back to their farm. While officers did indeed find evidence that shots had been fired from inside the house, there was nothing to suggest that anything had been hit. Likewise, police found no evidence of any creatures or strange lights, either in the sky or on the ground. The police left but later learned that the Sutton family claimed the creatures returned to the house again that night.

When news of the event hit the news wire, the Sutton farmhouse was overrun with police officials, reporters and locals, all wanting to hear more about what happened or, better yet, see one of those mysterious creatures for themselves. Of course, with each retelling, the events of that evening grew more bizarre, and it wasn't just the Sutton family who were elaborating and adding more details. The press started exaggerating everything from the number of creatures that attacked the house to the description of the creatures themselves. In fact, the Hopkinsville-Kelly case (so named because while the Sutton family went to the police station in Hopkinsville, their farm was in Kelly, Kentucky) marks the first time the phrase "little green men" was used to describe aliens from another world, even though the creatures were said to have silvery skin or wearing a silver suit.

Today, the Hopkinsville-Kelly case stands as one of the most controversial and polarizing events in ufology. Skeptics will claim that it was either a case of mass hysteria brought on by a night of drinking or an outright hoax perpetrated by some of the Sutton family members, who allegedly worked for a traveling circus and thought it would be funny to unleash a few live monkeys into the night. Believers point to the fact that if this were a hoax, why would the Sutton family, who kept to themselves, drive to a police station, knowing that once the story got out, they'd no longer be able to live a quiet, isolated life. But the biggest thing believers point to is that in 1955, people across the United States were reporting strange lights in the sky and encounters with small, humanoid creatures. It's at this point that our story begins creeping back to Ohio.

In 1955, ufologists Leonard Stringfield, Isabel Davis, Ted Bloecher and Bud Ledwith were investigating the Hopkinsville-Kelly event when they started to come across similar reports from around the area. As they continued their research, they found that the sightings and encounters were not limited to Kentucky. Crossing over into Ohio, the group was made aware of a reported 1955 sighting of several alien-like creatures "under a bridge" near Loveland, Ohio (likely where the idea of the Loveland Frog being spotted under a bridge originated). While interviewing Loveland police chief John K. Fritz about the encounter, he mentioned an unrelated incident where he was woken up at his house at 4:00 a.m. by someone pounding on his front door. When he opened it, he found Robert Hunnicutt, a man Fritz was familiar with, looking "as if he'd seen a ghost."

Chief Fritz went on to say that Hunnicutt told him that while he was driving home from work, he encountered several strange creatures standing alongside the road and that one of them held up a rod that emitted sparks. Fritz told the ufologists that he believed Hunnicutt and saw no evidence that he had been drinking or was under the influence. In fact, Fritz decided to follow Hunnicutt back out to the scene of the encounter, although he found nothing there. Upon hearing Chief Fritz's story, the ufologists made plans to interview Robert Hunnicutt.

On September 1, 1956, Hunnicutt was interviewed by the ufologists and even directed Leonard Stringfield in drawing a sketch of what he witnessed that night. According to the detailed notes, which were first published in 1978 by the Center for UFO Studies, while Hunnicutt couldn't recall if his encounter happened in late March or early April 1955, his mind remained clear on exactly what he witnessed that night.

Hunnicutt recounted that he was driving home from work, traveling north on the Madeira-Loveland Pike near "the vicinity of Hopewell Road at Branch Hill in Symmes Township." At approximately 3:30 a.m., Hunnicutt's car had topped a hill and was coming down the other side when his headlights caught several figures in the grass along the right side of the road.

"My first impression," Hunnicutt told the ufologists, "was that there were three crazy guys praying by the side of the road." When pressed for an explanation as to why he thought the men were praying, Hunnicutt said that was due to the figures, while appearing to be human, were smaller than the average adult male. In other words, he thought they were kneeling alongside the road.

Hunnicutt brought his car to a stop about ten feet away "to see what gives," but he kept his headlights focused on the strange scene in front of him. He even got out of his car, which is when he said he began to see and realize that these were not men kneeling alongside the road.

As Hunnicutt described them, the figures weren't kneeling—they were short, three to three and a half feet tall. There were three of them, all standing in what looked to Hunnicutt to be a triangular pattern, with the one closest to the road in front and the two standing behind on either side of the one in front. All three were one uniform grayish color. Hunnicutt said that if they were wearing clothing, it was extremely tight-fitting, as the color of their bodies matched that of their heads. Regarding their heads, while normal-sized, they all looked to be bald, although they appeared to have what looked like rolls of fat running vertically across them, which Hunnicutt likened to the way some dolls have painted-on hair. As for the faces, Hunnicutt's description and the ufologists' remarks are, in this author's opinion, what would cause this encounter to become linked to the Loveland Frog sightings decades later.

In the ufologists' notes, when it came to Hunnicutt ("the witness") describing the mouths of the three creatures, the following is noted (emphasis mine): "A large, straight mouth, without any apparent lip muscles, crossed nearly the entire portion of their faces—*an effect which reminded the witness of a frog*." It is interesting to note that this is the only "frog" reference in Hunnicutt's recounting, and yet it's the one that people latched onto.

Hunnicutt would go on to say that the feature that struck him most about the creatures were that the chests of all three of them were incredibly lopsided with what appeared to be swelling or a large bulge extending from under their right armpit all the way down to their waist.

As Hunnicutt stood there, trying to make sense of what he was looking at, the creature closest to him, the one in front of the other two, raised its arms a foot or so above his head. According to Hunnicutt, the creature appeared to be holding a rod or chain over his head—a rod that suddenly began to emit blue sparks. The creature then began to lower the rod, at which point Hunnicutt decided it was time to go. He got back in his car and sped off, but not before noticing an overpowering odor of what he described as a combination of "fresh-cut alfalfa with a slight trace of almonds." The entire encounter, in Hunnicutt's mind, lasted only about ninety seconds. He said his main reason for leaving and driving to the police chief's house was to get someone else to come out and witness the scene, which, as we've already learned, did not work out as planned. To date, no explanation has been given as to who or what Hunnicutt encountered alongside the road outside of Loveland, Ohio, that night.

There you have it: the genesis of the Loveland Frog legend, except the 1955 encounter had nothing to do with a creature that looked like a frog. It was merely the mouth that reminded Robert Hunnicutt, the witness, of a frog. Looking at the Hunnicutt description, you can see how some elements such as the creatures' height, over time, got woven into the 1972 description, causing it to literally grow from lizard size ("three feet long") to small, humanoid size ("three feet tall"). But in a side-by-side comparison, they are not the same creature. So, it would appear that the only confirmed sighting of the creature that would become known as the Loveland Frog happened in March 1972 and that those descriptions lean toward the animal being smaller and closer to, and acting like, an actual known species of reptile.

Now, if we could only explain away exactly what the creatures were that Hunnicutt spotted alongside the road in 1955, we'd be on to something. Clearly, they weren't Loveland Frogs. But what were they and where did they go? And what was the idea of holding up a sparks-emitting rod?

THE PHANTOM OF OXFORD

"He vanished into thin air!" You hear that all the time in movies and mystery novels. But things like that don't happen in real life, do they? A person can't just be there one minute and gone the next, seemingly into thin air, right? Especially in a public place or somewhere with lots of people around. Unfortunately, it does. And in the case of Ronald Tammen, he disappeared from his dorm room almost seventy years ago, leaving behind not a single trace of what happened or where he went.

Ronald Henry Tammen Jr. was born in Lakewood, Ohio, on July 23, 1933. Growing up, Ronald was the second of five children to parents Ronald Sr. and Marjorie, so there were always goings-on at the Tammen household. Looking back, there's absolutely nothing in Ronald's upbringing that would even hint at the strangeness that would soon follow. In fact, many people looked at Ronald Tammen as being something of a complete package: he was smart, got good grades and was athletic, eventually landing on the wrestling team, and he also had a musical side, playing the bass fiddle.

After graduating high school, Ronald Tammen applied to and was accepted at Miami University in Oxford, Ohio. In his freshman year at Miami University, Tammen made the Honor Roll with a GPA of 3.2, although he did appear to be suffering a bit of a "sophomore slump," and his current GPA was dipping down a bit. Aside from his studies, Tammen was also involved in extracurricular activities, most notably as the bass fiddle player in a campus jazz band called the Campus Owls. Tammen was also a member of the varsity wrestling team and had recently accepted a bid to join the Delta Tau Delta fraternity.

In the spring of 1953, Tammen was living in Fisher Hall, a freshman dorm on campus. Although he himself was a sophomore, he was allowed to live in Fisher because he was working there as a residence hall counselor. Tammen shared room 225 with fellow classmate Charles Findlay.

Even though spring was well underway, Sunday, April 19, 1953, was a cold one in Oxford, Ohio, with temperatures close to freezing and snow flurries throughout the day. Ronald Tammen had returned to Miami University late Sunday afternoon, having spent the day with the Campus Owls at a Cincinnati studio, recording several songs to be used for their submission to a *DownBeat* magazine contest.

A timeline constructed after the fact confirmed that Tammen returned to Fisher Hall late Sunday afternoon and was seen in his room "studying" as well as in other Fisher Hall rooms, helping people with their homework. There were also reports of Tammen being seen heading back toward his room with fresh linens. No one in Fisher Hall could remember seeing Ronald Tammen any time after 8:00 p.m. Sunday evening.

Tammen's roommate, Charles Findlay, was away from campus, spending the weekend at home in Dayton. When he returned to campus, it was late Sunday evening (an investigator's notes states that Findlay returned at 10:30 p.m.). Findlay said that when he got to room 225, the door was open and all the lights were on, but Ronald Tammen wasn't there. Looking around the room, Findlay saw that all Tammen's effects, including his wallet and car keys, were on his desk. There was even an open textbook there. Tammen's bed also appeared freshly made, although the pillowcases were missing. To Findlay, it seemed as though Tammen had just stepped out for a bit, maybe to visit with someone down the hall. But after waiting about an hour for his roommate to return, Findlay went to bed, leaving the lights on for Tammen.

Monday morning, when Charles Findlay woke up in room 225, he found everything exactly as it had been when he went to sleep, right down to Ronald's light still being on. All Tammen's personal effects were still there, too, untouched. Even Tammen's bed remained made up. Still, Findlay didn't feel like there was any cause for alarm, thinking that perhaps Tammen had a last-minute decision to spend the night at his fraternity house, Delta Tau Delta. So, Charles got dressed and went off to class, making a mental note to check in at the fraternity house later.

Miami University's Marcum Center, built on the spot where Fisher Hall once stood.
Author photo.

Later that day, upon meeting with Tammen's fraternity brothers and finding that Tammen hadn't spent the night at the frathouse, Findlay became concerned. Heading back to Fisher Hall, Findlay started asking around to see if anyone had seen or heard from Ronald. Some said they had seen him inside Fisher Hall Sunday evening, but by 9:00 p.m., Ronald Tammen had seemingly simply vanished. Fearing the worst, Charles Findlay alerted Miami University staff that his roommate was missing.

It should be noted that in the 1950s, campus security was not what it is today. The idea of a student disappearing while on campus was not something Oxford University had much experience with, so the person sent out to do the initial investigation of room 225 and interview the residents was not a detective, police officer or security guard. It was Miami University's dean of men, Dr. Carl W. Knox.

When Dr. Knox first arrived at Fisher Hall, he began his investigation by examining room 225. Inside, he found everything in its place and confirmed with Charles Findlay that all Tammen's personal effects were exactly where they had been when Findlay returned Sunday evening. Knox could find no evidence of a struggle having taken place in the room, although he did question why the door to room 225 was open when Findlay returned. Findlay stated that since Tammen was a residence hall counselor, he would always leave the door open, only closing it if he was leaving campus or going to sleep. That statement led Knox to believe that if Tammen had left the room of his own accord that Sunday evening, he wasn't planning on going far. Knox also noted that Tammen's bed did not appear to have been slept in and was made up with what appeared to be new bedding, all except for the pillow, which had yet to have a new pillowcase put on it.

Examining Tammen's desk, Knox located Tammen's wallet, which contained all the important things someone would take with them if they were leaving—driver's license, ID card, even his draft card. Tammen's car keys were also found. One of the perks of being a residence hall counselor was that Tammen was given a parking spot at Fisher Hall. Peeking outside, Knox found Tammen's car was still parked outside. When the car was investigated later, it was found to be locked with Tammen's bass safely inside. As with room 225, there were no signs of a struggle detected inside or around Tammen's car. A final intriguing item on Tammen's desk was an open psychology book. The fact that the book was open led Knox to surmise that Tammen had been studying just before he left room 225.

Knox next began interviewing the other residents of Fisher Hall to see if anyone remembered seeing Ronald Tammen on the night of Sunday, April 19. There were several who did indeed see him, with the latest sighting taking place right down the hall from room 225, in room 212, where Tammen was helping a student with their homework. Knox noted that while he was in room 212, Tammen appeared to be in "good spirits."

Remembering the new bedsheets he saw on Tammen's bed, Knox went to speak with Ora Todhunter, Fisher Hall's residence hall manager, to see if she recalled seeing the young man. Todhunter did indeed recall seeing and interacting with Ronald Tammen on April 19. She told authorities that around 8:00 p.m., Tammen came down from his room and asked for two sheets, a pillowcase and a mattress cover. Todhunter said Tammen looked tired, and when she commented on that, Ronald said he was tired and was planning on going back to his room and straight to bed.

While speaking with Ora Todhunter, something strange came to light— something that would fuel conspiracy theories for decades: Tammen needed to change his sheets because someone had put a dead fish in his bed. But despite the images of mobsters threatening Tammen that he'd "sleep with the fishes" if he didn't change whatever he was doing, or that it had something to do with his disappearance, the fish in the bed, while strange, has a normal explanation: it was put there by some "freshmen pranksters."

Knox next reached out to the Delta Tau Delta fraternity house as well as Tammen's brother, Richard, who was a freshman at Miami University and was living on campus in Symmes Hall. None could provide any information about Ronald's current whereabouts. Finally, Knox was forced to contact Ronald's parents, who also had not seen their son recently and did not know where he could be. It was then that Knox began to suspect that something was terribly wrong.

When a thorough investigation of the entire Miami University campus yielded no clues and few leads, the decision was made to involve agencies outside the university. While Carl Knox would continue to head up the investigation as it pertained to Miami University, the Oxford Police Department also opened an investigation, with Police Chief Oscar Decker taking the lead. This was done to follow up on any leads that might suggest Tammen was no longer on campus property and was instead somewhere in Oxford, Ohio.

Within a week of Tammen's disappearance, multiple search parties, consisting of not only law enforcement but also Tammen's friends, fraternity brothers and even four hundred air force ROTC cadets, took to scouring miles around Fisher Hall in every direction. *Miami Years* recalled that the woods "three miles above and below Fisher Hall" were searched, as were the shores of Hueston Woods' Acton Lake, which is more than five miles from campus. When an old cistern was found behind Fisher Hall, it was drained, but no evidence was found. On Sunday, April 26, almost all of Heuston Woods' three thousand acres were searched. Still, there was no sign of Ronald Tammen.

As with any mystery without any clues, rumors as to what happened to Ronald Tammen quickly began swirling around Miami University: he was the victim of foul play and dragged down the fire escape near room 225; he had a case of amnesia and simply wandered away; or he was trying to hide from someone (or something) and had planned his own disappearance to start a new life. Among the most persistent stories was that Tammen had been dating a girl from Hamilton, Ohio (some said she was from Indiana), and that on the night of his disappearance, Tammen had been seen sitting in the girl's car, which was parked outside of Fisher Hall, and that the pair eventually drove off together. Who this woman was, or if she ever really existed, has never been confirmed. But the idea that Tammen might have traveled outside Oxford and Butler County, Ohio, was what fueled local authorities to broaden their search by getting first the Ohio State Highway Patrol and then the FBI involved. By the end of April 1953, a "five-state alarm" had been issued and all bus, railroad and airport terminals had been searched in all five states adjoining Ohio—Michigan, Indiana, Kentucky, West Virginia and Pennsylvania. Still, no Ronald Tammen.

A little more than two months after Tammen's disappearance, on June 29, 1953, an article ran in the *Journal Herald* newspaper that possibly provided the first real lead in the case. According to the article, Police Chief Oscar Decker said that a woman had stepped forward, claiming to have seen Ronald Tammen the night he disappeared.

That woman was Clara Josephine Spivey, who lived with her family on North Main Street in Seven Mile, Ohio, a village roughly eleven miles to the east of Oxford. According to Clara, she had recently read an article about Ronald Tammen in the local newspaper, and when she saw the photo of Tammen that accompanied the article, she was reminded of an incident that took place at her home, close to midnight on April 19. Clara said there was a knock at the front door, and when she answered it, she was met by a young man whom Clara was now certain was Ronald Tammen. She was immediately struck by how the man did not appear appropriately dressed for the weather. But then Clara noticed a dirt or grease smudge on the young man's face; she took that to mean that perhaps the man was having car trouble. But rather than ask to use the phone, the young man on the doorstep asked questions like "What town am I in?"—leading Clara to believe that he was lost. The stranger also never mentioned that he was in any sort of trouble or that anything had happened to him. In fact, after getting general directions to the closest bus line, the young man simply thanked Mrs. Spivey and walked off into the darkness.

Today, walking from Fisher Hall to the Spivey home in Seven Mile would take you close to three and a half hours, and that's if you stick to the main roads. Keeping in mind that Ronald Tammen was last seen shortly after 8:00 p.m. inside Fisher Hall, he would have had to have walked nonstop to make it onto Clara Spivey's doorstep at the time she reportedly saw him. So, it seems highly unlikely that the person she encountered really was Ronald Tammen, even if she was a little off on the time. However, Spivey's story can't be dismissed entirely if one considers that perhaps Tammen didn't *walk* to Seven Mile from Oxford and was instead just trying to get back to Miami University after having been driven off campus to an unknown location. Local authorities followed up on Clara's statements, but no trace of Ronald Tammen or anyone matching his description was uncovered in Seven Mile

Right: Welcome to Seven Mile, which might be the last place Ronald Tammen was seen alive. *Author photo.*

Below: Seven Mile's Main Street. If that was Ronald Tammen on Clara Spivey's doorstep in 1953, this is the route he likely took. *Courtesy of Courtney Willis.*

or anywhere along the way from Seven Mile to Oxford or even Hamilton. Regardless, Clara Spivey never wavered from her assertion that the person was Ronald Tammen, even when others disagreed.

The years rolled on with no movement in the case and not a single confirmed sighting of Ronald Tammen. Authorities began to put forth the theory that Tammen had suffered a bout of amnesia and simply wandered away from campus. But Tammen's family and friends swore that Ronald had never had amnesia before or exhibited any symptoms. Plus, if it had been amnesia, how was he able to get so far away from campus that a search across five state lines failed to uncover a single clue? For this reason, many began to suspect foul play. This theory, however, felt weak because there were no signs of a struggle inside Tammen's room or around Fisher Hall, and no one reported hearing any sort of argument on the night Tammen disappeared that he could have been part of. On top of that, Ronald Tammen was well liked and did not appear to have had any enemies.

There were some who believed that Tammen had wanted to disappear and simply walked off to start a new life somewhere. Again, there's nothing in Tammen's past that would suggest this, and perhaps most telling of all, Tammen left everything behind in his dorm room, including money and uncashed checks. Likewise, the money in his account at a local Oxford bank remained untouched for years, eventually being closed out and the money given to Ronald's parents.

In the 1960s, with many beginning to believe that Ronald Tammen was deceased, people began seeking alternative means by which to attempt to ascertain exactly what happened that April night in 1953. "Professional mediums" were brought onto campus, often conducting séances to packed houses, to attempt to contact the spirit of Ronald Tammen. Most were unsuccessful, but one claimed to have received a vision of a young man who, upon hearing "loud noises," left his second-floor room and descended to the basement, where he encountered "two men of evil," who attacked him. The vision faded as the two men carried the young's man's body outside. This particular "vision" seems to have taken hold and continues to make its way across the Internet even today, despite the logistics involved for it to have happened that way are slim to none, right down to two men dragging a body out of the basement area without being seen by any of the students or staff in the building at the time.

The next possible clue to Ronald Tammen's disappearance would not appear until shortly after the twentieth anniversary of his vanishing. On Monday, April 23, 1973, the *Journal-News* published an article by Joe Cella titled "County Coroner Says Oxford Officials Ignored Data on Missing Miami Student 20 Years Ago." In the article, Butler County physician and coroner Dr. Garret J. Boone claimed that Ronald Tammen visited his Hamilton, Ohio office on November 19, 1952—five months prior, to the day, that Tammen disappeared. Dr. Boone stated that the reason for the visit was because Tammen wanted to have a test to get his blood typed. Tammen was informed that Dr. Boone's office did not perform such tests, and the young man was referred to nearby Mercy Hospital for the lab test. Boone was able to produce the office record of Tammen's visit and even posed with it for the photo that accompanied the newspaper article.

When asked why he waited so long to come forward with this information, Boone replied that he had tried to give the information to "local authorities at the time, but it was always discounted." Boone then went on to imply that his getting the brush-off was perhaps part of a conspiracy, but he refused to elaborate, stating only, "I believe somebody knows something about this case, but they don't want to be involved."

Boone believed that Tammen's visit to his office for a blood type test was somehow connected to his disappearance and that Ronald Tammen was still alive…somewhere. "I don't believe he is dead," Boone told reporter Joe Cella, "and people in the Oxford area don't want to be involved." In an "Editor's Footnote" to the story, Joe Cella concurred with Dr. Boone's opinion that Ronald Tammen was still alive: "I don't believe Tammen is dead. I never did. I have my own thoughts about this case." Cella, who kept a photo of Ronald Tammen in his wallet since the student's disappearance, continued to research and write about the case until he passed away in August 1980. At the time of his passing, Cella had yet to make his theories about the Ronald Tammen case public.

In 1978, Fisher Hall was abandoned and slated for demolition. After everything was removed from the building, a top-to-bottom search was conducted for any sign of Ronald Tammen's remains. None was found. When Fisher Hall finally came crashing down, another search was done through all the rubble, but again, nothing was found. Several years later, in September 1982, the Marcum Center, a hotel and conference center, opened on the spot where Fisher Hall once stood. But while the building might not have been there anymore, Fisher Hall's legacy and Ronald Tammen's memory lingered on. Even today, there are stories of a shadowy figure walking around outside the Marcum Center, said to be Ronald Tammen's ghost, and of strange things happening inside the Marcum Center "where Tammen's room would have been."

In early 2008, nearly fifty-five years after Ronald Tammen disappeared, Butler County detectives received what many hoped was the break they were waiting for. Cold case detectives in Walker County, Georgia, had reached out to the Butler County Sheriff's Office with information about an unsolved murder case they had, involving an unidentified male that possibly matched the description of Ronald Tammen.

In late June 1953, the body of an unidentified young white male, approximately five-foot-ten, with dark hair and a muscular build, was found murdered along U.S. 27 near Lafayette, Georgia, in Walker County. Wearing only a T-shirt and shorts, it was estimated that the body had been there at least a month, which would put the young man's murder taking place only a few weeks after Tammen's disappearance. But perhaps most intriguing of all was that the body was found near U.S. 27, which runs straight through Oxford, Ohio.

Butler County detectives found that since the murder victim was never identified, he was buried at Lafayette's city cemetery, which meant that if they could get a DNA sample from one of Ronald Tammen's brothers or sister, they could exhume the body at the cemetery and compare DNA to confirm once and for all if this person was Ronald Tammen.

Armed with DNA from Ronald's sister, Marcia, detectives headed south to Georgia. In February 2008, the body was exhumed at Lafayette Cemetery and several bone fragments were collected; these were sent to the Georgia Bureau of Investigation for comparison against the Tammen DNA. Several months later, the results were made public: the unidentified man was not Ronald Tammen. Along with the news, Walker County sheriff Steve Wilson released a statement, which read in part, "Our hearts go out to the Tammen family who have been searching for answers concerning their loved one for 55 years."

As of this writing, we are quickly approaching the seventieth anniversary of the night Ronald Tammen walked out of his room at Fisher Hall and disappeared. We appear to be no closer to solving the mystery, as there appears to have been little, if any, movement in the case since 2008. The amazing website A Good Man Is Hard to Find—My Search for Ronald Tammen, created and maintained by Jennifer Wenger, is a virtual storehouse of all things related to Ronald Tammen and serves to help keep the case alive while also offering new theories to be explored regarding Tammen's disappearance. That's as it should be—after all these years, Ronald Tammen's family and friends still deserve answers. And Ronald Tammen should never be forgotten.

SOUTHERN OHIO UFO FLAPS

When there are multiple sightings of an unidentified flying object reported in one geographic area over a short period of time, UFO researchers refer to that as a "flap." Unlike traditional UFO sightings that involve either a single witness or two to three individuals, flaps often involves dozens of witnesses, making it harder to dismiss that there was something strange in the sky. Such is the case with two UFO flaps involving southern Ohio, where dozens of witnesses, including police officers and a commercial pilot, saw things in the sky that to this day have yet to be fully explained.

One of the first major UFO flaps to involve southern Ohio happened on Monday, July 12, 1965. The reports first started coming in the midafternoon: a round, light-colored object that "appeared to be made out of a plastic material" in the skies over Harrisburg, Pennsylvania, moving to the southwest. By 6:00 p.m., the same object was seen over Columbus, Ohio, and Lockbourne Air Force Base near Columbus was able to track the object, estimating that it was at about sixty thousand feet. As the sun went down on the twelfth, the object became more visible in the sky, and more reports came in from all southern Ohio, with a heavy concentration of calls coming from Hamilton, Ohio residents. Something strange happened as the object moved into southern Ohio: the round, light-colored object was now being described as "elongated" and orange in color. The FAA flight service station at Morgantown, West Virginia, would later claim that the orange object was "hundreds of feet" in diameter and appeared to be at an altitude of close to ninety thousand feet. The following day, Wright-Patterson Air Force Base admitted that it was tracking the object but had "no idea what the object was."

So, what was it? Like most UFO sightings, skeptics would claim that what people were seeing was either the ever-popular "Fall Planet," Venus; a very bright star; the dreaded weather balloon; or, to explain the object's reported difference in color and shape, *two* weather balloons, even though most weather balloons at the time were roughly six feet in diameter and not known to reach altitudes the unknown object allegedly did.

Strange as the 1965 flap was, it would pale in comparison to the October 1973 event, where strange objects were reported over the skies of southern Ohio for more than a week. What's more, not only were civilians making the reports, but reporters and police officers were seeing something as well.

The flap began on the evening of Wednesday, October 10, with the first report coming in at approximately 8:00 p.m. from the village of New

UFO Shadowed In Ohio: Balloon, Star, Or What?

An example of the media coverage for the 1965 Southern Ohio UFO Flaps. *From the* Cincinnati Enquirer, *Tuesday, July 13, 1965.*

Lebanon. Over the course of the next twelve hours, there would be at least sixteen reports of a strange object in the night sky, with some sightings involving groups of witnesses. According to Montgomery County sheriff's deputy Michael Sullivan, an unnamed officer in New Lebanon witnessed an oblong-shaped object covered with red, green and blue lights hovering just above the trees. The officer said that he remained in his patrol car and continued to observe the object for several minutes as it continued to hover. The officer then decided to shine his car's spotlight at the object, at which point, according to Sheriff's Deputy Sullivan, the officer claimed the object "zoomed towards him and then shot straight up in the air."

When news of this sighting hit the morning papers, more people started coming forward, alleging that they, too, had seen something strange in the sky. Sheriff's Deputy Sullivan now added that they had a report of a strange object in the sky that had been "visible for some 30 minutes to about 25 residents gathered on a city street." Sullivan added that the subsequent sightings stretched from New Lebanon Township down toward Cincinnati and that the sightings lasted from "a fleeting moment" to close to twelve minutes. One local paper named "New Lebanon Patrolman Robert Bales" as one of the witnesses. While Bales might be the "unnamed officer" from the initial report, the details of the sighting have changed, so he might not be the same guy. For example, the "Bales" encounter describes "four bright lights" that were moving across the sky and then dropping down to treetop level, where they disappeared.

A final reported sighting of this object came in the early morning hours of Thursday the eleventh. The Ohio Highway Patrol responded to a call from a woman who said there was a "multi-lighted object" in the sky. The officer arriving on scene found close to fifty people standing outside, all claiming to have seen something in the sky, but the object had left the area. The officer remained in the area but was unable to locate the object. When reached for comment about the incidents, Wright-Patterson Air Force Base would only say that on the night in question, nothing anomalous was detected on radar.

After Thursday's predawn sightings, the objects appeared to disappear completely. And as southern Ohio rolled through the weekend with nary a

15 UFO Sightings Are Reported in One Night in Southwest Ohio

sighting, it appeared as though whatever had been up in the sky was gone for good. In fact, they were only getting started.

On Monday, October 15, the reports began almost as soon as the sun went down. The first calls were from the Trenton area, reporting strange objects of various shapes and colors moving around in the sky. While most of the initial reports were of the objects being high in the sky, several were like the earlier New Lebanon sightings in that the objects were reported as dropping down to treetop level. In fact, Trenton police were sent out to investigate the report that "a UFO had landed" on or near Main Street. Upon arrival, police were unable to find any evidence of anything out of the ordinary. But the reports were only beginning to come in.

Springdale's Keith Merrill reported that he and four other individuals stood outside the Tri-County Shopping Center and observed a strange object in the sky for close to twenty-five minutes. Merrill, a commercial pilot, said that the object "hung in the sky to the east" and that it would occasionally fade, only to reappear moments later. Merrill was also able to observe the object with binoculars, noting that what looked like a simple "bright light" to his naked eye "seemed to have a hazy blue light around its middle" when viewed through binoculars.

From his Milford backyard, seventeen-year-old Bryan Werring watched as a red, white and blue object moved in an easterly direction while "flying parallel to the moon." While over on Kirkland Drive in Finneytown, eleven-year-old Warren Smith was hanging out with his friend, thirteen-year-old Jeff Fossett, when around 9:35 p.m., the pair looked up and saw a "bright ivory light" in the sky. Smith described the object as looking like a five-pointed star. Subsequent sightings of a similarly shaped object started coming in from Delhi Township and Mount Lookout. Some news outlets began reporting that witnesses said they saw something "star-like" in the sky, leading many skeptics to surmise that the object was nothing more than an actual star.

Shortly before 10:00 p.m., a listener called in to Portsmouth radio station WPAY and told newsman Dan Robbins about something strange in the night sky. After getting specifics about where the object was located, Robbins was able to see it for himself. Robbins would later claim that he saw an object streaking across the sky, leaving a "white trail in the sky" as it moved toward the east. Robbins was able to observe the object for almost three minutes before it disappeared. After it left, Cincinnati police began taking the first of several reports of the same strange light in the sky, but by the early morning hours of October 16, the object had once again vanished.

The final incident in the October 1973 flap occurred shortly after midnight in Athens, Ohio, on Thursday the eighteenth. Unlike previous nights, the objects observed remained in the skies over one specific location, Athens, and were not seen anywhere else. While there were only three witnesses, all were Athens city police officers and were able to observe the objects for almost ninety minutes.

The first object was spotted over the Lakeview Apartments by the three officers at 12:55 a.m. They described a white object that looked like "an ice cream cone" surrounded by small white lights that were "similar to falling stars." They estimated that the object was at an altitude of approximately ten thousand feet and was moving in an easterly direction toward the "Old Airport" on East State Street. Upon reaching the airport, the object hovered above it for approximately thirty minutes before it began moving in a southwesterly fashion until it disappeared over the horizon. Including the thirty minutes they watched the object hovering, the officers stated that they were able to observe the object for an astonishing forty-five minutes.

As soon as the first UFO vanished, the officers claimed that it was "replaced" by a second UFO. This one had a similar ice cream cone shape as the first UFO, but more cylindrical. It also appeared to be much higher in the sky, but as it was hovering directly overhead, the officers had a hard time gauging its altitude. This object emitted a bright light that one of the officers compared to starlight but added, "It was much brighter than any other stars." While the object hovered, the officers did not hear it emitting any sound, but they noticed that its light would "fade out for about five minutes" before becoming very bright again, which they took to mean that the object was rotating. The officers were able to observe this object for approximately thirty minutes before clouds rolled in and obscured it from view. When detailing their accounts to reporters, the officers stated that they were so intrigued by what they were witnessing that they went so far as to try signaling both UFOs by flashing their spotlights on their patrol cars at the objects. Unfortunately, in both instances, the object failed to respond.

And with that, the 1973 Southern Ohio UFO Flap was over. So, what exactly was going on in the skies of southern Ohio? Almost immediately, skeptics announced that it was one of the usual suspects: the planet Venus or a weather balloon. But not so fast. Those explanations become problematic when you line up all the descriptions of the object and find that they are too varied to conclude that all the witnesses were seeing the same object. During the 1973 flap, witnesses described three distinctly different shapes—round, five-pointed star and "ice cream cone." So, it appears there were several objects in the skies of southern Ohio in October 1973.

The notion of multiple objects becomes problematic for skeptics, who simply want to throw a blanket "it was Venus" or "just a weather balloon" over the entire weeklong flap. This is a case of one size (or shape) does not fit all. A weather balloon could potentially be the explanation for the ice cream cone–shaped object, but the five-pointed star? This is what leads some skeptics to declare that the witnesses saw Venus some nights and a weather balloon on other nights. Aside from being a bit absurd, we must consider that while it is certainly possible some people mistook something "normal" in the sky, the 1973 flap is chock full of trained witnesses such as police officers and even a commercial pilot, who would be well aware of what normal things in the night sky look like.

What do I think was going on? Honestly, I have no idea. I'm willing to discard some of the accounts as misidentifications or just plain hoaxes/pranks, but I'm still left with a handful of reports from trustworthy sources. There's much more to this flap, I know it, so I'm going to keep digging. As of today, I'm calling what people saw in October 1973 UFOs because they fit the definition: they're unidentified, they were flying and they were objects. I'll keep you posted and let you know if my research turns up anything to contradict that definition.

In the meantime, if you ever find yourself driving through southern Ohio on a dark October evening, be sure to take a moment and take a quick peek at the sky. You never know what you might see moving around up there.

PART VI
LEGENDARY EVENTS

BUCKEYE BELLE EXPLOSION

In the nineteenth century, prior to the arrival of the railroad, the preferred method of moving mail, products and people throughout southeastern Ohio was the Muskingum River. Formed in northeast Ohio by the confluence of the Tuscarawas and Walhonding Rivers, the Muskingum flows south, past the city of Zanesville, before reaching the Ohio River at Marietta. Seeing the potential of this river, the Ohio government created the Muskingum River Improvement Project in 1836. The purpose of this project was to make it easier to navigate the Muskingum by installing a series of locks and dams designed to control the level of water. Plans also called for the creation of a canal near Dresden, Ohio, that would allow boats to move from the Muskingum over to the Ohio and Erie Canal, further expanding the reach of ships traveling on the Muskingum. The project was completed in 1841, and soon thereafter, boats of all shapes and sizes were making their way up and down the Muskingum River.

One of the immediate impacts the Muskingum River Improvement Project had was on the delivery of mail in Ohio. While the traditional way of sending mail at the time was via stagecoach, putting mail on board a boat in Marietta, Ohio, often meant that it could arrive in Zanesville, in central Ohio, within a few hours or sooner if the boat were fast enough. This led to a rush to build the biggest and fastest boats capable of navigating the Muskingum River.

At the time, boats didn't get bigger or faster than the steamboat. These giant, multi-decked boats were perfect for the Muskingum, as they were large enough to carry freight and passengers while still being small enough to navigate the river itself. Steamboats got their name from what made them go: steam. To create the steam, giant metal containers known as boilers would be filled with water. Using coal, fires would be started under the boilers, which caused the water to reach its boiling point, creating steam. That steam would then be pumped over to a cylinder, which had a piston at the bottom of it. As the steam rose within the cylinder, so did the piston. Opening a valve on the cylinder would allow the steam to escape, causing the cylinder to drop back down to the bottom. By connecting the other end of the piston to a propellor or paddle wheel, its constant up-and-down motion would create the force to move the boat. Of course, if you wanted to go faster, things got a bit more dangerous—bigger fires to make the boilers hotter to create more steam, which would have to get released faster. It was a recipe for disaster but deemed a necessary evil if one was to compete for work on the Muskingum River.

In May 1852, a new steamboat splashed into the Muskingum River from the Knox Boatyard in Marietta: the *Buckeye Belle*. The *Belle* was a side-wheeler steamboat, meaning its paddle wheel was on its side as opposed to sternwheels, which had their wheel at the stern, or back, of the boat. It had been designed large enough to fit a full crew with plenty of room for mail, freight and passengers. Its two large boilers meant that the *Buckeye Belle* was built for speed. While it would occasionally take on special assignments, the *Belle*'s regular task would be delivering mail between Marietta and Zanesville, which it would do on a tri-weekly basis.

On the afternoon of November 12, 1852, the *Buckeye Belle* was out on the Muskingum River, having left Marietta, heading for Zanesville on one of its regular runs. The boat was passing through Lock no. 4, located along the village of Beverly, when suddenly, a loud explosion shook the area. Residents who came out of their houses were horrified to see what was left of the *Buckeye Belle* fully engulfed in flames. But there was hardly anything left of the boat to speak of. Most of it was now floating in the Muskingum or littering the shoreline. Drawing closer, it became apparent that among the debris were human remains. Incredibly, residents were able to locate a few survivors among all the carnage and immediately began tending to the wounded. The grave task of trying to identify the deceased also began, which quickly proved problematic, as most of the remains were not intact—in some cases, only pieces of bodies were located. Above all was the mystery of what exactly happened to the *Buckeye Belle*.

Lock 4 today. *Author photo.*

In the 1850s, news didn't travel as fast as it does today. And when it did, it was often full of inaccuracies. The first reports of the *Buckeye Belle* explosion came via a "telegraphic dispatch from Marietta" and ran the following day in the November 13 edition of the *Daily Zanesville Courier*. The newspaper reported that the *Buckeye Belle* had "burst or collapsed her boilers, by which accident 15 persons were killed," even though back in Beverly, people were still literally sorting through body parts and attempting to locate unaccounted-for passengers and crew members. Additionally, while issues with the boilers seemed to be the obvious choice for the cause of the explosion, twenty-four hours after the incident, nothing had been confirmed. This caused further issues when other local newspapers picked up the story and began adding their own embellishments, including making accusations of "recklessness" on the part of the engineer, the one responsible for the boat's boilers.

With news as terrible as the explosion of a steamboat came the idea that people would want to read about all the gory details, and local newspapers began having a field day with just that. While there is no doubt that the scene in Beverly was truly horrific, one must question the validity of such newspaper reports as the tongue of a victim being found on the banks of the

By the National Line.

TELEGRAPHED FOR THE DAILY INTELLIGENCER

Awful Explosion of the Steamboat Buckeye Belle!

Sixteen Killed!---A Number Wounded!

TOTAL DESTRUCTION OF THE BOAT!

One of the first newspaper accounts of the *Buckeye Belle* explosion. *From the* Wheeling Daily Intelligencer, *Monday, November 15, 1852.*

river, severed heads being located along the hillside "still wearing hats" and, in my personal favorite bit of weirdness, "a rabbit was killed by the fall of a brick, nearly 400 feet from the boat."

But what exactly happened aboard the *Buckeye Belle*? Since there was no *CSI: Beverly* in existence to conduct the investigation, it was decided that with so many deaths, the incident should be handed over to a coroner's jury, a group usually brought together to determine cause of death. After examining the remains of the *Buckeye Belle*, including the boilers, the jury found that the explosion was the result of an excessive build-up of steam pressure in the boilers. This was caused, the jury concluded, because the *Belle*'s second engineer, Joseph Daniels, had been negligent in not opening the valve that would have allowed the steam to escape. This seems logical, but conspiracy theorists point to the fact that the jury felt the need to add this statement to the official findings: "During our examination, we are happy to say, that the officers of the boat have been completely exonerated from any blame." Was the jury attempting to cover up what really happened on the *Belle* by making Daniels, who survived the explosion, the fall guy for everything? Regardless, while the jury found Daniels at fault for the explosion, there are no records indicating that he was ever prosecuted or punished for anything related to the *Buckeye Belle* explosion.

The coroner's jury also provided what at the time was believed to be the most accurate number of fatalities related to the explosion itself. Of the forty-five known people on the *Buckeye Belle* on November 12, 1852, the jury found that twenty-one of them, including five who could not be identified, died in the initial explosion. Three more individuals would later succumb to injuries sustained in the explosion, including newly elected Ohio governor Cassius C. Covey. The official record is that twenty-four of the forty-five people aboard the *Buckeye Belle* died because of the explosion.

Of course, depending on which resource you consult, the number of people killed ranges from fifteen to thirty. Part of the reason for this was because there was no real accurate count of how many people were

Historical marker at Lock 4 in Beverly. *Author photo.*

on board that day. There were the registered crew and passengers, of course, but it was not uncommon for people to stow away for one reason or another. To add to the confusion was the inability to identify all the recovered remains. In some instances, a single hand or foot was all that was found, which led to a "box" of assorted human remains that were never identified. It is said that the box was buried at nearby Beverly Cemetery. Years later, a monument was erected in this cemetery that would add further confusion to the *Buckeye Belle* disaster. The monument was paid for by Edward Matthews Ayers, grandson of the *Buckeye Belle*'s captain, Harry Stull. A plaque on the monument states that it was erected "to the memory of these unknown dead and also to Captain Harry Stull." The plaque also notes that "here lie buried thirteen unknown persons, killed by the bursting of the boiler of the Steamer *Buckeye Belle*." It is unclear where Ayers got the number thirteen from.

As for the *Buckeye Belle* itself, while hardly anything remained of it, at least intact, the decision was made to rebuild it. Less than two years after her explosion, the *Buckeye Belle* was back on the river, and by 1857, it had graduated from the Muskingum River and was making its way up and down the mighty Mississippi River. But two weeks after the fifth anniversary of its explosion, November 26, 1857, the *Belle*'s boilers once again exploded near Columbus, Kentucky. Even though there were no fatalities in this explosion, the decision was made to not rebuild the *Buckeye Belle* again.

A final intriguing postscript to the *Buckeye Belle* tale concerns the boat's safe, which, on the day of the explosion, was said to contain $1,500 (valued at more than $53,000 today). When reports began circulating that the safe was not recovered from the debris and was considered missing, treasure seekers from all over Ohio descended on Beverly, looking for the safe. Over time, the amount the safe supposedly had inside it continued to grow until there were whispers that it contained "untold riches." Even when the safe was found nineteen years later, in 1871, by fishermen J.W. Truesdall and G.C. Barkhurst, the legend of the *Buckeye Belle*'s riches refused to die. That's because, according to reports from 1871, there was nothing inside the safe, which showed signs of having "been opened long before." So, where did the money go? Some believe that the safe was blown open in the explosion and that its contents were scattered along the banks of the Muskingum River or else sank to the bottom, where it all sits today, waiting to be found.

USS *Shenandoah* Crash

During World War I, the German military unleashed a new weapon on Great Britain: zeppelins—giant, blimp-like flying machines consisting of fabric covering over a rigid, metal framework. Germany discovered that zeppelins—originally looked on as slow-moving and therefore useless in times of war—could be made to fly higher than any ground anti-aircraft fire or enemy planes could go, making them ideal for surveillance and bombing runs. In October 1917, the German zeppelin L-49 went off course and was forced to land, intact, in France. Almost immediately, every country, including the United States, wanted a peek inside to see what made it tick.

As early as 1920, there were whispers about the U.S. Navy researching ways to improve on the L-49 zeppelin. In 1922, the navy began construction on its very first rigid airship, ZR-1, at Naval Air Station Lakehurst (NAS Lakehurst) in New Jersey. When completed, ZR-1 was massive in size: 680 feet long, with a diameter of 79 feet. In addition to the main structure, there were several "gondolas," which hung below the main structure and housed ZR-1's engines. There was also a large gondola that hung from the center of ZR-1, sometimes referred to as the control car, where the commander could check navigation and issue orders. Altogether, the ZR-1 tipped the scales at a whopping thirty-six tons, not including crew. It should be noted that this weight was after the navy had made a conscious effort to build the ZR-1 lighter than other zeppelins to allow it to rise faster—a move that reduced the overall strength of the structure.

A major difference between the ZR-1 and its German counterpart was the gas used to make it rise. German zeppelins used highly flammable hydrogen gas, which was stored on board in gas cells. Releasing the hydrogen from these gas cells was what allowed the zeppelin to descend, making the area around the structure flammable too. While the ZR-1 was constructed with twenty gas cells, capable of holding 2,115,000 cubic feet of hydrogen, the decision was made to switch to helium gas when the *Roma*, an Italian semi-rigid airship the U.S. Air Force was taking on a test flight, burst into flames when the hydrogen it was carrying caught fire, killing all thirty-four crew members on board.

The first official flight of ZR-1 was on September 4, 1923—a test flight from its home base in NAS Lakehurst, New Jersey. Following several other successful test flights, the ZR-1 was officially christened the USS *Shenandoah* on October 10, 1923. Legend has it that the name was chosen because it means "daughter of the stars." Truth be told, the "daughter of the stars" legend is also associated with the Shenandoah River, except that version says the word *Shenandoah* means "clear daughter of the stars." That, as well as the fact that the three other rigid airships built at NAS Lakehurst were all named after towns/cities (USS *Los Angeles*, USS *Akron* and USS *Macon*), calls the Shenandoah legend further into question.

Regardless of where its name originated, the USS *Shenandoah* continued to make successful fights for the next two years. The initial trips served as on-the-job training for this new type of flying machine, including the crew getting used to using helium as opposed to hydrogen. But the crew took to the *Shenandoah* quickly, and before long, the ship was on promotional tours across the United States, showing everyone how the new age of air travel had arrived. And with a range of several thousand miles, there seemed to be nowhere the *Shenandoah* couldn't go!

On the morning of September 2, 1925, the *Shenandoah* was scheduled to leave NAS Lakehurt for its fifty-seventh flight—a promotional appearance in St. Louis with stops in Minnesota and Michigan before returning to New Jersey. The *Shenandoah* had recently taken on some new crew members, including a brand-new skipper, Greenville, Ohio native and U.S. Navy lieutenant Commander Zachary Lansdowne. As Lansdowne reviewed the weather forecasts along the route the *Shenandoah* planned to take, he noticed that there was a good chance of encountering some severe thunderstorms over southern Ohio. Perhaps due to his being born and raised in Ohio and therefore familiar with the unpredictability of Midwest thunderstorms and their penchant for causing severe windstorms, Lansdowne attempted to postpone the flight until the storms passed. When he was overruled, the USS *Shenandoah*, with its crew of forty-three men, lifted off from NAS Lakehurst, heading for St. Louis.

September 2 passed into September 3 without incident as the *Shenandoah* made its way west. Hours before dawn, the *Shenandoah* passed into southern Ohio, cruising along at an altitude of approximately 2,700 feet. From his spot in the control car, Lieutenant Commander Lansdowne could see lightning flashes in the distance, indicating that they would be heading into a storm in several hours. Lansdowne never had time to prepare his crew for the storm, however, because at 5:25 a.m., the *Shenandoah* ran into a current of warm air, causing its nose to rise and the entire ship to begin a rapid ascent, carried upward by the current. At one point, the nose of the *Shenandoah* had risen so far that members of the crew felt as if the entire ship was now flying perpendicular to the ground, all while it continued to rise higher and higher, tossed about by the wind.

Lansdowne had to quickly decide how to get the *Shenandoah* back under control, and he immediately called for the valves on the gas cells to be opened. Lansdowne believed that releasing the helium gas would stop the ship's ascent, bringing the nose back down in the process.

When the *Shenandoah* had reached an altitude of 4,600 feet, a climb of almost 2,000 feet, the ship stabilized and the nose dropped back down, so the gas cell valves were closed while the crew continued to stabilize the ship. Opening the valves had helped, but the ascent had also been slowed because the *Shenandoah* had passed through that blast of warm air. For several minutes, the *Shenandoah* remained at 4,600 feet, rocking back and forth as the winds swirled around the ship. Then the *Shenandoah* was hit from below by another violent burst of wind, and the ship once again began to climb.

Just as before, Lansdowne ordered the gas cell valves open, but this time, the crew couldn't get them open. The *Shenandoah* quickly reached heights of more than seven thousand feet, and the winds began to literally bend the internal structure of the ship. Lansdowne ordered several men in the control car back to assist in getting the valves open. Shortly after that, a loud cracking noise was heard as the control car broke free of the *Shenandoah*, sending it hurtling down to the ground, splitting the *Shenandoah* into two pieces in the process.

Left: Stone memorial at crash site no. 1, the spot where the *Shenandoah*'s control car fell to the ground. *Author photo.*

Below: The bow section of the *Shenandoah*, where it came to rest after breaking apart. *NH 98998, courtesy of the Naval History & Heritage Command.*

Honolulu Star-Bulletin

Last Edition

14 PAGES—HONOLULU, TERRITORY OF HAWAII, THURSDAY, SEPTEMBER 3, 1925—14 PAGES ★★★ PRICE FIVE CENTS

14 DIE IN U. S. DIRIGIBLE WRECK

While the *Shenandoah* crashed in the early morning hours of September 3, by midafternoon news had already spread. *From the* Honolulu Star-Bulletin, *Thursday, September 3, 1925.*

As the control car crashed to the ground, killing everyone on board, including Lieutenant Commander Zachary Lansdowne, the two remaining pieces of the *Shenandoah* began drifting, rather than falling, to the ground. The stern section, which, after the control car broke free, amounted to the rear two-thirds of the ship, about four hundred feet long, glided into the ground, tail up, about half a mile from where the control car crashed. Incredibly, all the men in this section survived.

The bow portion of the *Shenandoah*, with seven crewmen inside, continued to climb and drift to the south. Incredibly, crewmen were able to vent the helium from the remaining gas cells, bringing the bow back down toward the ground. About forty-five minutes later, the bow of the *Shenandoah* had descended low enough that the crewmen began throwing out lines, hoping that they would snag something on the ground, allowing them to climb down. As the bow crossed over the farmland of Ernest Nichols, Nichols was able to grab one of the lines and tie it to a tree. Some of the men climbed down on the line and, borrowing a shotgun from Nichols, were able to shoot the gas cells, releasing the helium and bringing the bow down. The last piece of the USS *Shenandoah* had finally landed.

While fourteen men lost their lives on September 3, 1925, the idea that the *Shenandoah* had forty-three men aboard when it broke apart thousands of feet in the air and there weren't more lives lost is nothing short of miraculous. The fourteen men who lost their lives that day were:

- Everett Allen
- Charles Broom
- James Cullinan
- Lewis Hancock
- Arthur Houghton
- Ralph Joffray
- Zachary Lansdowne
- Jack Lawrence
- Celestino Mazzuco
- James Moore
- Bart O'Sullivan
- George Schnitzer
- Edgar Sheppard
- William Spratley

Sign erected at site no. 3, where the bow of the *Shenandoah* came to rest. *Author photo.*

The *Shenandoah* disaster led to many changes in the construction of rigid airships. In addition to building them stronger, they were also outfitted with powerful engines to enable the ships to outmaneuver storms. Perhaps the biggest improvement to come out of the disaster was a revamping of the weather forecasting system the military uses.

Left: Memorial to the USS *Shenandoah* in Ada, Ohio. *Author photo*.

Right: The "Landowne" stone at crash site no. 1. *Author photo*.

Today, monuments have been erected at all three crash sites—the control car ("Crash Site 1"), the stern ("Crash Site 2") and the bow ("Crash Site 3"), as well as one memorial placed in Ada, Ohio, near the spot. Crash Site 1 also contains an object whose true purpose may have been lost to time. It is a small, flat stone, into which someone has etched, "This is the spot of the Landowne." Most believe the stone marks the spot where the body of Zachary Lansdowne was recovered. Others point out that Lansdowne's name is misspelled on the stone and has "the" in front of it, leading to the belief that the carver overheard Lansdowne's name and mistook it as the name of the *Shenandoah*, which would mean the stone marks the spot where the control car fell. Regardless of what it marks, the stone is yet another touching memory to the collective memorial for the USS *Shenandoah* in Southeast Ohio.

THE WHO CONCERT DISASTER

It's Monday, December 3, 1979, and southern Ohio is abuzz with excitement: The Who were in town for a concert at Cincinnati's Riverfront Coliseum (now known as the Heritage Bank Center) in support of their 1978 release, *Who Are You.* There were many reasons for everyone to be excited for this show. Not only was this The Who's first tour since the passing of their original drummer, Keith Moon, on September 7, 1978, but it would also mark the band's first show in Cincinnati since 1975.

Excitement was so high that when tickets went on sale months earlier, it was a complete sellout—18,348 tickets—in under two hours. Of all the tickets sold, less than 20 percent of them were for reserved seats. The overwhelming majority were considered General Admission, often referred to as festival seating. What that meant was your ticket got you into the venue and you were free to grab seats (or a spot on the floor to stand) as close to the stage as you wanted. Of course, that usually meant getting to the venue hours ahead of time, before the doors were opened, and then having to run, push and shove to get to the front of the stage before all the other General Admission ticket holders beat you there. That's why, shortly after noon on December 3, fans began showing up outside the Coliseum, even though the show was not scheduled to start until 8:00 p.m., meaning the Coliseum doors would be locked until at least 6:30 p.m.

During the afternoon, various rumors started making their way across southern Ohio: a "local radio station" had announced that all General Admission ticket holders were going to be admitted around 3:00 p.m. to hear a special sound check by The Who. There was going to a special surprise opening act: The Who were going to offer a special screening of their newly released film, *Quadrophenia*, before the show. Regardless of which rumor people heard, one thing was abundantly clear: if you had tickets to the show, you needed to get down to Riverfront Coliseum ASAP. By midafternoon, several thousand ticket holders had crowded into the plaza area on the western side of the coliseum, near the sixteen doors that comprised the main entrance. While there were reports of the usual pre-concert debauchery taking place in the crowd, there was no hint of the impending tragedy.

But as the sun went down and the temperature started to dip down toward freezing, the crowd, which had swelled to an estimated size of more than seven thousand people, began pushing their way toward the still-locked west entrance doors. Police were sent out to the front of the crowd to get them away from the doors in anticipation of their opening, but they had little effect as the mass of people began crowding in tighter and tighter.

While the doors were supposed to be opened at 6:30 p.m., the appointed time came and went, and they remained closed. Lieutenant Dale Menkhaus, who had been out in the crowd, managed to locate one of the promoters,

Cal Levy, and asked him if they could open the doors to start letting people in. Levy said the doors needed to remain closed since The Who, who had performed the previous night in Pittsburgh, had not yet completed their pre-concert sound check. Apparently, there were also issues about having enough ticket takers to cover the entrances. So, for now, the doors needed to remain closed. All the while, the crowd outside continued to grow larger and more impatient.

By 7:00 p.m., the crowd had grown so large—some estimates went as high as twelve thousand people—that the entire plaza outside the coliseum was almost packed solid. While the initial plan had been to open all sixteen doors at once, this quickly proved impossible as the doors all opened outward and the crowd had collectively pushed themselves up against the locked doors. So, police and security staff began trying to get the crowd moved back so that the doors could be opened, with limited success. In fact, they were only able to get two of the sixteen doors open, both being located on the far right side of the main entrance. Those near the two open doors began to push and fight their way through, while others in front of the closed doors tried to push their way over to the openings. Suddenly, there was a mighty surge as the entire crowd seemed to be slammed up against the entrance doors. The chaos had begun.

There are conflicting reports as to why the crowd suddenly surged forward. Some people claimed that others in the crowd heard The Who inside the coliseum doing their sound check and mistook that to mean the concert had begun. Others said it was simply that people were trying to be among the first to get inside to score a prime spot from which to watch the concert. Whatever the reason, by 7:15 p.m., thousands of fans outside the coliseum had turned into one giant mass of humanity, violently ebbing and flowing against the doors of the building. People near the locked doors were being crushed against the glass, while those in the crowd who fell to the ground were being trampled over. Unable to get any of the remaining locked doors open, fans smashed a hole in one of them, and people began crawling through the broken glass to escape the crowd.

Police and medical staff on site were immediately notified that there were injuries in the crowd but were initially unable to get through to help. Calls went out for backup, and it is said that by the end of the night, every rescue EMT and paramedic unit in Cincinnati had been dispatched to the Coliseum. Incredibly, through all this madness, most of the fans were able to eventually make their way inside the coliseum, while EMTs began tending to the wounded. The first body was located at 7:45 p.m.

11 concertgoers die at Cincy coliseum

News of the tragedy spread quickly. *From the* News Herald, *Tuesday, December 4, 1979.*

Inside Riverside Coliseum, The Who and their manager, Bill Curbishley, had no idea of the tragedy that was unfolding outside. In fact, Curbishley stated that he had no idea anything was wrong until after The Who had taken the stage and were several songs into the show. Curbishley said that when he was told there was a "problem up on the plaza level," he went to see for himself and was horrified at what he saw: bodies of deceased fans being taken away while EMTs worked feverishly to help those injured. This was the main reason why when he was approached by Cincinnati fire marshal Clifford Drury and made aware that they were considering canceling the show, Curbishley refused. He feared that if the show were canceled, another riot would break out inside the Coliseum. Plus, people exiting on the west side of the Coliseum would be walking right into the area where police and medical personnel were trying to treat the wounded.

As for the band itself, Curbishley made the decision to wait until after The Who were finished playing to tell them what had happened. The only thing he told them was that when it came time for the encores, they should only play two songs because "we've got a real serious problem." So, after The Who performed "Summertime Blues" and "The Real Me," Curbishley gathered the band together and told them there had been an incident outside where people had been killed and injured.

"We didn't know what to say or do," guitarist Pete Townshend would say, years after the event. So, since the band had a show the following evening in Buffalo, New York, they made the decision to leave Cincinnati and head for New York, a decision that Townshend says he regrets doing. "We should have stayed."

Numbers related to how many fans were injured vary, since many of them were treated at the scene and released. Twenty-five people sustained injuries that required them to be transported to the hospital. However, the most sobering statistic of all is that on December 3, 1979, eleven individuals lost their lives while waiting to attend a concert:

- Walter Adams Jr., aged twenty-two, Trotwood, Ohio
- Peter Bowes, aged eighteen, Wyoming, Ohio
- Connie Sue Burns, aged twenty-one, Miamisburg, Ohio

- Jacqueline Eckerle, aged fifteen, Finneytown, Ohio
- David Heck, aged nineteen, Highland Heights, Kentucky
- Teva Rae Ladd, aged twenty-seven, Newtown, Ohio
- Karen Morrison, aged fifteen, Finneytown, Ohio
- Stephan Preston, aged nineteen, Finneytown, Ohio
- Phillip Snyder, aged twenty, Franklin, Ohio
- Bryan Wagner, aged seventeen, Fort Thomas, Kentucky
- James Warmoth, aged twenty-one, Franklin, Ohio

As soon as reports of the tragedy hit the news wire, people wanted answers. More importantly, they wanted to know who was responsible and how this was able to happen. Initial reports made mention of The Who continuing to perform on stage, even as the tragedy continue to unfold outside the coliseum, leading to the obligatory comparisons to Nero playing his fiddle while Rome burned. Once people realized that the band had been unaware of what was going on and that there was nothing The Who could have done to prevent the tragedy, attention quickly turned to the idea of festival seating events creating potentially volatile situations at rock concerts due to fans clambering for front-row views. This led Providence, Rhode Island mayor Vincent "Buddy" Cianci to cancel The Who's December 17 show at the Providence Civic Center, even though the venue did not offer festival seating, only assigned seats. On December 27, 1979, the City of Cincinnati announced that it was imposing a ban on all "unassigned festival seating" events, a ban that would remain in place until the early 2000s.

In 1983, a class-action suit filed against The Who, Electric Factory Concerts (the concert promoter) and the City of Cincinnati on behalf of ten of the eleven families of the deceased was settled. The family of the eleventh victim, Peter Bowes, elected to not participate in the class-action suit and instead sued individually. That suit was also settled out of court.

Rock fans crushed
11 killed in Ohio stampede for 'The Who'

Headlines such as this left everyone searching for answers as to how this could have happened. *From the* Billings Gazette, *Tuesday, December 4, 1979.*

Singer suggests group return for Cincy concert

Mere days after the tragedy, band members already realized that they needed to return to Cincinnati. *From the* Telegraph-Forum Daily Tribune, *Saturday, December 15, 1979.*

Something that is often overlooked in reports on this tragedy is the impact it had on the Cincinnati suburb of Finneytown. Three Finneytown High School classmates—Jackie Eckerle, Karen Morrison and Stephan Preston—all lost their lives outside Riverfront Coliseum on December 3, 1979. Nearly thirty years later, in 2009, fellow Finneytown High School alums Steve Bentz and John Hutchins decided that something needed to be done in memory of their classmates. They were able to raise enough funds to place a memorial bench bearing the names of their three classmates in front of the Finneytown High School's Performing Arts Center on August 21, 2010. But Bentz and Hutchins didn't stop there. They teamed up with another Finneytown High School alum, Fred Wittenbaum, and the three created the P.E.M. Memorial (Stephan Preston, Jackie Eckerle and Karen Morrison), which gives out scholarships to Finneytown High School students pursuing a degree in the arts. To date, more than thirty scholarships have been given out. As for the memorial bench, the area around it has been expanded to include memorial plaques to the three Finneytown High School students and a brick plaza.

In 2012, The Who announced that they would be making a tour stop at the Providence Civic Center (now named the Dunkin' Donuts Center) the following year, marking their first return to the venue since their canceled 1979 show. The venue then announced that anyone who presented a ticket for the canceled 1979 show at the ticket office could exchange them for tickets to the 2013 concert. Incredibly, several individuals did just that, turning in their 1979 tickets for ones to The Who's February 26, 2013 show. The 1979 tickets were then turned over to Rhode Island Special Olympics, which auctioned them off as memorabilia.

In December 2014, on the eve of the thirty-fifth anniversary of the tragedy, Cincinnati mayor John Cranley announced plans to have a memorial historical marker erected in front of Riverfront Coliseum (which had since been renamed the U.S. Bank Arena). The following year, on December 3, 2015, a double-sided marker was unveiled outside the arena. The front of the marker has the date of the tragedy and a brief description, with "Eleven in Memoriam" on the back, along with the names, ages and hometowns of the eleven individuals who lost their lives.

As for The Who, they have yet to return to Cincinnati for a concert. In 2019, the band announced what was touted as The Who's first return to Cincinnati since the tragedy (although it was to take place at BB&T Arena in Kentucky, just across the Ohio River), to be held on April 23, 2020. The COVID-19 global pandemic forced the band to postpone the show, and as of this writing, a new date has not been announced. But if Pete Townshend has anything to say about it, The Who will be back in Cincinnati sooner rather than later, something he made perfectly clear in a recent documentary about the tragedy. "We need to go back to Cincinnati," Pete Townshend said.

Postscript: Just as this manuscript went to press, The Who announced dates for their 2022 *The Who Hits Back* tour. Gone is the Kentucky date, replaced by one for Sunday, May 15, at TQL Stadium in Cincinnati.

SELECTED BIBLIOGRAPHY

Abbott, Karen. *The Ghosts of Eden Park*. New York: Crown, 2019.

Airships.net. "ZR-1 U.S.S. *Shenandoah*." https://www.airships.net/us-navy-rigid-airships/uss-shenandoah.

Alter, Maxim. "Living in a Murder House: Hamilton Mom Copes with Her Home's Dark Past." WCPO. https://www.wcpo.com/news/local-news/james-ruppert-easter-sunday-massacre-hamilton-woman-copes-with-living-in-a-murder-house.

Athens Messenger. "Athens Policemen Spot 2 UFOs." October 18, 1973.

Billings Gazette. "Rock Fans Crushed." December 4, 1979.

Brinkmoeller, Tom. "Girl Seen Entering Car: 2 Sought for Quiz in Stabbing." *Cincinnati Enquirer*, September 6, 1976.

———. "Who's Daltry Feels Helpless, Guiltless." *Cincinnati Enquirer*, December 5, 1979.

Brock, Ira. "UFO Sightings Come Fast and Furious." *Cincinnati Enquirer*, October 16, 1973.

Brooklyn Daily Eagle. "The Open Pole Theory: First Advance by Captain John Cleves Symmes." February 9, 1896.

Buchanan, Tyler. "Tishman's Tale." *The Messenger*, October 29, 2017.

Carbone, Mariel. "Memorial Honored Finneytown Students Killed at The Who Concert Years Ago." WCPO. https://www.wcpo.com/news/local-news/hamilton-county/finneytown/memorial-honored-finneytown-students-killed-at-the-who-concert-40-years-ago.

Carpenter, Amelia. "Trail to the Truth: The Ron Tammen Mystery 58 Years Later." *Miami Student*, April 22, 2011.

Cella, Joe. "County Coroner Says Oxford Officials Ignored Data on Missing Miami Student 20 Years Ago." *Journal-News*, April 23, 1973.

———. "Why Did Tammen Disappear Forever?" *Journal-News*, April 18, 1976.

The Chattanoogan. "Exhumed Body Is Not Missing Ohio Student." June 20, 2000. https://www.chattanoogan.com/2008/6/20/130149/Exhumed-Body-Is-Not-Missing-Ohio-Student.aspx.

Cincinnati Enquirer. "Eugene Is Buried, Dead Since 1929." October 21, 1964.

———. "Eugene Laughs Last! OSU Chills Corpse's Kidnappers—Only Pride of Sabina Is Resting." December 5, 1958.

———. "Loveland's Castle Builder Severely Burned." March 17, 1981.

———. "Two Years Pass Without a Trace of Oxford Student." April 20, 1955.

———. "UFO Shadowed in Ohio: Balloon, Star, or What?" July 13, 1965.

Conlon, Kevin. "The Who to Return for Makeup Concert—33 Years Later." CNN, February 26, 2013. https://www.cnn.com/2013/02/26/showbiz/music/the-who-concert-redo/index.html.

Cook, William A. *King of the Bootleggers: A Biography of George Remus*. Jefferson, NC: McFarland, 2008.

Cubarrubia, Eydie. "It Went Bump in the Night." *The Post*, October 31, 1991.

Cummings, James. "Crop Circle Pops Up." *Dayton Daily News*, September 10, 2004.

Daily Press. "29-Year-Old Ohio Corpse Disturbed by Pranksters." November 12, 1958.

Daily Reporter. "Convicted Killer Escapes Ohio Pen." February 23, 1970.

Daily Times. "Identify Students Expelled at OSU." December 6, 1958.

Daniels, Sue. "Halloween: Here's Local Ghost Story." *Lancaster Eagle-Gazette*, October 30, 1986.

Davis, Isabel, and Ted Bloecher. *Close Encounters at Kelly and Others of 1955*. N.p.: Flying Disk Press, 2018.

Dayton Daily News. "Decade Later, Where's Ronald?" April 18, 1963.

———. "Eternal Roadside Resting Place" April 11, 1992.

———. "14 Years Later—Where's Ronald Now?" April 19, 1967.

———. "Miami Student Still Missing; Four Years Pass, No Clues." April 19, 1957.

———. "Stees Guilty of Killing Wife." February 10, 1963.

———. "Youth's Fate Still Puzzles Police Chief." December 29, 1954.

Dobie, Sara. "Misleading Story of Athens Upsets Residents." *The Post*, November 9, 2000.

Doe Network. "Ronald Henry Tammen." http://www.doenetwork.org/cases/1562dmoh.html.

Elkins, Bob. "Loveland's 'Knight' Dies, Leaves Castle to Millions." *Cincinnati Enquirer*, April 17, 1981.

Ellis, Bill. *Aliens, Ghosts, and Cults: Legends We Live*. Jackson: University Press of Mississippi, 2003.

Escanaba Daily Press. "Remus Found Not Guilty of Murder." December 21, 1927.

Fleeman, Michael. "Roy Rogers, King of the Cowboys, Dead at 86." *Daily Spectrum*, July 7, 1998.

Gallipolis Journal. "Terrible Steamboat Explosion." November 25, 1852.

Garbee, Pat. "Woman Attractive to UFOs." *Dayton Daily News*, December 1, 1978.

Gill, Richard. "The Headless Motorcyclist." *Ohio Folklore Society Journal* (December 1972).

Go Fish Ohio. "Dow Lake Fishing Map." https://gofishohio.com/ohio-fishing-information/dow-lake-fishing-map-southeast-ohio.

Goldstein, Jan. "In Loveland Frog'll Boggle Minds." *Journal Herald*, April 12, 1972.

Grace College. "About Grace College." https://www.grace.edu/about.

Great Parks of Hamilton County. "Richardson Forest Preserve." https://www.greatparks.org/parks/richardson-forest-preserve.

Harris, C.H. "Many of These 13 Cemeteries Were Family Burial Grounds." *Athens Messenger*, March 1, 1956.

Hatfield, Sharon. *Enchanted Ground: The Spirit Room of Jonathan Koons*. Athens, OH: Swallow Press, 2018.

Havigurst, Walter. *The Miami Years: 1809–1984*. New York: G.P. Putnam's Sons, 1958.

Hawk, Ira Gossett. "Ohio's Mystery Man." *Columbus Citizen*, January 12, 1947.

Heller, Ann. "Guns: James Rupert Liked to Collect Them, Now They Say He Used Them to Kill 11." *Journal Herald*, April 1, 1975.

Honolulu Star-Bulletin. "14 Die in U.S. Dirigible Wreck." September 3, 1925.

Hunter, Al. "The Ghosts of Kings Island, Part 1." Weekly View, May 16, 2013. http://weeklyview.net/2013/05/16/the-ghosts-of-kings-island-part-1.

Janssen, Volker. "How the 'Little Green Men' Phenomenon Began on a Kentucky Farm." History.com. https://www.history.com/news/little-green-men-origins-aliens-hopkinsville-kelly.

Jones, Richard O. "Solid Rock Church Dedicates Statue." *Dayton Daily News*, October 1, 2012.

Journal Herald. "Clue Renews Hope." June 29, 1953.

Journal-News. "What Happened to Ronald Tammen? Mystery Unresolved After 18 Years." April 22, 1972.

Kazanjian, Howard, and Chris Enss. *The Cowboy and the Senorita: A Biography of Roy Rogers and Dale Evans*. Guilford, CT: TwoDot, 2017.

Kelly, Michael. "Marietta's The Anchorage Gains New Life on Haunted History Tours." *Parkersburg News and Sentinel*, March 16, 2018.

Krajicek, David J. "The 1975 Easter Massacre: Uncle Jimmy Ruppert Kills His Family." *Daily News*, April 3, 2010.

Kurtzman, Lisa. "Oxford's Mystery Man Revived." *Cincinnati Enquirer*, January 19, 2008.

Lawson, Fred. "Motive Unknown in Deaths." *Journal Herald*, April 1, 1975.

Leggate, James. "Officer Who Shot 'Loveland Frogman' in 1972 Says Story Is a Hoax." Wcpo. https://www.wcpo.com/news/local-news/hamilton-county/loveland-community/officer-who-shot-loveland-frogman-in-1972-says-story-is-a-hoax.

Logan Daily News. "Gene Stees Convicted." February 11, 1963.

———. "OU Professor Pleads Innocent." October 26, 1962.

Loveland Castle. "Historic Loveland Castle & Museum." https://lovelandcastle.com.

Marietta Times. "Touring the Anchorage." https://www.mariettatimes.com/news/2017/12/touring-the-anchorage.

Martin, Jean. "Notables Dot Athens' Past." *Athens Messenger*, August 28, 1977.

Marysville Journal-Tribune. "FBI Joins Hunt for Missing Son." May 18, 1953.

McCauley, Byron. "The Who Concert: Cincinnati Anchor Tanya O'Rourke Explores New Ground." USA Today, December 2, 2019. https://www.usatoday.com/story/news/politics/columnists/2019/12/02/who-concert-wcpo-anchor-tanya-orourke-covers-new-ground/4309903002.

McCrabb, Rick. "Solid Rock Still Growing After Leader's Death." *Dayton Daily News*, December 2, 2012.

The Messenger. "Three Killed in Head-On Crash." March 8, 1970.

Miami University. "Ron Tammen Disappearance." https://www.miamialum.org/s/916/16/interior.aspx?pgid=417.

Mulligan, Ann. "Spooks Haunt Area Hills and Valleys." *Athens Messenger*, October 26, 1969.

Murphy, Kate. "'Finally': Marker for 11 Killed at The Who Concert." N.d. Cincinnati. com.

News Herald. "11 Concertgoers Die at Cincy Coliseum." December 4, 1979.

News-Messenger. "Ohio University Professor, Murder Trial Principal, Could Have Lost Sanity: Doctor." February 8, 1963.

Ohio Department of Rehabilitation & Correction. "Most Wanted." https://drc. ohio.gov/wanted.

O'Reilly, Molly. "Local Lore Found on Library Shelves." *Lancaster Eagle-Gazette*, October 31, 1991.

Palladium-Item. "Easter Reunion Ends in Death for 11 at Hamilton." March 31, 1975.

Palm Beach Post. "UFO Flap Jolts Residents." October 12, 1973.

Patterson, Emily. "Five Athens Cemeteries Form Lopsided Square." *The Post*, October 30, 2003.

Pitman, Michael D. "Fireworks Show Planned for Jesus Statue Dedication." *Journal-News*, August 17, 2012.

Portage Sentinel. "Heart-Rending Calamity." December 29, 1847.

The Province. "Ohio UFO Snapped." October 12, 1973.

Riverboat Dave's. "About Buckeye Belle." http://www.riverboatdaves.com/ aboutboats/buckeye_belle.html.

Robin, Josh "What Happened to Utopia?" *Spectrum News*, April 26, 2019. https:// spectrumnews1.com/oh/columbus/untangled-with-josh-robin/2019/04/26/ what-happened-to-utopia--oh.

Robinette, Eric. "Solid Rock Founder Dies." *Dayton Daily News*, October 2, 2011.

Robinson, Amelia, and Dave Larsen. "Statue's Sculptor Would Like to Help Rebuild It." *Dayton Daily News*, June 16, 2010.

Rogers, Roy, and Dale Evans. *Happy Trails*. New York: Bantam Books, 1981.

Rolling Stone. "10 Who Fans Redeem Canceled 1979 Rhode Island Concert Tickets." https://www.rollingstone.com/music/music-news/10-who-fans-redeem-canceled-1979-rhode-island-concert-tickets-182233.

Rule, Leslie. *When the Ghost Screams*. Kansas City, MO: Andrews McMeel Publishing, 2006.

Scariest Places on Earth. "Satan's Dormitory." Season 1, episode 1. Fox Family, October 23, 2000.

Schaefer, Walt. "13 Violent Death in Area Still Unsolved." *Cincinnati Enquirer*, April 15, 1979.

Schneider, Norris F. "'Buckeye Belle' Explosion Occurred in Locks at Beverly 107 Years Ago." *Times Recorder*, December 13, 1959.

Sharkey, Mary Anne. "Held in 11 Deaths: Ruppert Competent, Experts Tell Court." *Journal Herald*, May 13, 1975.

Society for Psychical Research. "About the SPR." https://www.spr.ac.uk/about-spr.

Socol, Tony. "Boardwalk Empire Season 5: The Real George Remus." Den of Geek. https://www.denofgeek.com/tv/boardwalk-empire-season-5-the-real-george-remus.

Standish, David. *Hollow Earth: The Long and Curious History of Imagining Strange Lands, Fantastical Creatures, Advanced Civilizations, and Marvelous Machines Below the Earth's Surface*. Boston, MA: De Capo Press, 2006.

TIME. "Music: The Stampede to Tragedy." http://content.time.com/time/subscriber/article/0,33009,920746,00.html.

Times Reporter. "Body in Lake: Ohio U. Instructor Admits Slaying." October 26, 1962.

———. "Murder Trial Goes to Jury at Athens." February 9, 1963.

Trembley, Craig. *Guide to Ohio University Ghosts & Legends*. N.p.: Lulu Press Inc., 2007.

Tribune. "Exhumed Remains Not of Missing Student." June 21, 2008.

———. "Student Missing." April 26, 1953.

Walters, Sally. "We're 'Protected Against Evil'…but We Can Still Frighten You." *Athens Messenger*, October 27, 1977.

Washington C.H. Record-Herald. "Sabina's 'Eugene' Laid to Rest After 35 Years." October 21, 1964.

WCPO. "The Who: The Night that Changed Rock." Via YouTube. https://www.youtube.com/watch?v=RgGvPdrwQas.

———. "The Who Planning 2022 Return to Cincinnati." https://www.wcpo.com/news/local-news/hamilton-county/cincinnati/the-who-planning-2022-return-to-cincinnati.

Wenger, Jennifer. A Good Man Is Hard to Find—My Search for Ronald H. Tammen, Jr. https://ronaldtammen.com.

Wessa, Pauline. "Library Compiling the Chilling History of Fairfield Ghosts." *Columbus Citizen-Journal*, November 7, 1980.

Wheeling Daily Intelligencer. "Awful Explosion of the Steamboat Buckeye Belle." November 15, 1852.

Willis, James A. *The Big Book of Ohio Ghost Stories*. Mechanicsburg, PA: Stackpole Books, 2013.

———. *Ohio's Historic Haunts*. Kent, OH: Kent State University Press, 2015.

Willis, James A., et al. *Weird Ohio*. New York: Sterling Publications, 2005.

Wilmington News-Journal. "Kidnapped 'Eugene' Makes OSU Visit." November 11, 1958.

———. "Over Million Persons Have Seen 'Eugene' at Littleton's in Sabina." November 23, 1955.

Wilson, Denise. "Statue's Demise Draws Big Response." *Hamilton Journal-News*. June 16, 2010.

Wired.com. "Fantastically Wrong: The Real-Life Journey to the Center of the Earth that Almost Was." October 2010. https://www.wired.com/2014/10/fantastically-wrong-journey-to-the-center-of-the-earth.

Wisconsin State Journal. "15 UFO Sightings Are Reported in One Night in Southwest Ohio." October 12, 1973.

WKRC. "Memorial Held for Victims of The Who Concert Tragedy." https://local12.com/news/local/memorial-held-for-victims-of-the-who-concert-tragedy.

Woodyard, Chris. *Haunted Ohio*. Beavercreek, OH: Kestrel Publications, 1991.

ABOUT THE AUTHOR

J ames A. Willis has been walking on the weird side of history for close to forty years. When not out chasing after all things strange and spooky, Willis found the time to author more than a dozen books, including *Central Ohio Legends & Lore*, *Ohio's Historic Haunts: Investigating the Paranormal in the Buckeye State*, *The Big Book of Ohio Ghost Stories* and *Haunted Indiana*. He is also the director of The Ghosts of Ohio, a paranormal research group Willis founded in 1999.

A sought-after public speaker, Willis has given presentations throughout the United States, during which he has educated tens of thousands of people of all ages in crowd sizes ranging from ten to well over six hundred. He has been included in hundreds of media sources, including CNN, *USA Today*, *Midwest Living*, *Fox Sports*, the *Canadian Press* and the *Astonishing Legends* podcast.

Willis currently resides in Galena, Ohio, with his wife and daughter and two narcoleptic cats. He can often be found lurking around his virtual abode, strangeandspookyworld.com.